MW00938510

Purgatory

Heaven's Healing Waters

W.J. Novack

Cover design by W.J. Novack

Table of Contents

TABLE OF CONTENTS.. 2

ACKNOWLEDGMENTS.. 3

AUTHOR'S NOTES.. 5

WHAT IF I HAD DIED? 6

INTRODUCTION 17

HOLINESS 26

THE NATURE OF GOD 42

JOY & SUFFERING OF OUR WOUNDED HEARTS.........107

WHAT DOES THE CHURCH SAY? 116

FORGIVENESS OF SIN 120

THE FIRE OF THE HOLY SPIRIT 124

OUR CAPTURED HEARTS...128

OUR SUFFERING SAVIOR 149

FRUIT OF THE SPIRIT 155

PHYSICAL SUFFERING...177

JOY IN SUFFERING...180

WE SUFFER TOGETHER..185

OUR HOPE IN JESUS..189

PRAYING FOR THE DEAD...193

FINAL THOUGHTS 226

FOOTNOTES 241

END NOTES..253

Acknowledgments

~

Thank you, Father, our Lord Jesus Christ, and Holy Spirit for being my constant companions and a constant source of grace throughout my life. You love me even when I am unlovable. One of the ways in which you have best shown me your love is through the gift of my wife, Mary.

Mary, thank you for being Christ to me in so many ways throughout our 30 years marriage. You have loved me when I was unlovable and stood in the gap for me when I have been inconsolable. You are truly my most precious gift in this life. You are my best friend and lover. I could have never wished for a better partner to share in this journey. You are a consummate mother to our children, to our grandchildren, and even to many who are not our own. An outsider would never know the difference. I love the way you love. Thank you for sticking by my side. I love you.

Thank you to the folks who have helped and encouraged me throughout this process; to Father Tom Connery at St. Peters Catholic Church, in DeLand, Florida for his words of affirmation and encouragement; to Tim Gibson, my RCIA director when I came into The Church at Immaculate Conception Church, in Hendersonville, North Carolina, for his input, guidance, and help and encouragement throughout the daunting task of editing; to Bob Fitzpatrick who gave so willingly his time with proofreading and genuine desire to enrich the message, and for my editor Brittany Clarke of Copyediting by B. Clarke, for jumping right in, and also for her Protestant input and perspective.

Author's Notes

~

The translation of the Bible utilized in this writing is the New American Bible, Revised Edition (NABRE). This translation is widely used by Catholics and is readily accessible through the United States Conference of Catholic Bishop's web-site. The web address is www.usccb.org.

What if I Had Died?

~

"It comes. You know that It is not of yourself. It is from without, and It attaches Itself to your deepest parts. First comes loneliness, then abandonment, then despair, then the pain is so great you want It to end by any means. Just before you are crushed by the grip of It, there comes a trickle of love that can only come from the Divine. Then, It pours... no, It gushes in, without removing any of the pain. The volume of It's presence actually pushes the pain deeper into your being. Every cell of your body shares the pain with your heart. Your body, soul, and spirit collapse at His feet. You feel you don't have the strength to lift your fingers. Like discovering that you are in the middle of the ocean and realizing that you are standing on an inch of ice, without any earthly hope, a small part of you wishes it would break, while the rest of you is trying not to move, so you can stay alive. The ends of your fingers actually tingle with expectation. Now you wish without repentance that Whatever has entered your being would crush you and drag you back with It. You never want It to leave. Now It subsides, you feel It pulling away, and you grab for It in desperation. But,

there is nothing you can do to hang onto It. You cannot control It's coming, or It's going. You just know that you will spend the rest of your life longing for It above all else. You will never be the same. Then you realize, when It left, It took with It every bit of anger, shame, and resentment from who you are, because It has captured your heart. You want the whole world to have It, but It is not yours to give."

W.J. Novack

We are born into this world innocent and unable to protect ourselves, the most vulnerable of all its inhabitants. The god of this world, the devil, like a hungry wolf, attacks the most vulnerable. He is not only out to hurt humanity; he is out to drag humanity down into the pit that is waiting for him in hell; into eternal damnation, suffering, and separation from God. Our adversary wants nothing less than death for all of humanity.

My uncle molested me as a toddler. This attack on my life was a one-time event. My mother and father kept me safe from my uncle after that, but several like attacks continued to assail me from many directions throughout my childhood. I, along with millions of children in this country, grew up living with the consequences of the sexual revolution - the culture that coined the phrase *"free love"* and sang along to songs with lyrics like *"if you're not with the one you love, love the one you're with."* One of the biggest lies is that sex is free - that what we do behind closed doors does not hurt anybody. That is a lie perpetrated by the king of liars, the devil.

As I grew older, my idea of what it meant to be an adult was obviously skewed by the events of my childhood. I have never molested a child, but I have definitely perpetuated the sexual sin that plagues humanity. I often think of sin as a web, a snare in which we are so very easily entangled. As we fight to become free of its painful grip, we shake the web and entangle others.

As a young adult, I attempted to stuff the shame of my childhood deep within myself in the hope that it would just go away. The deeper I stuffed the pain, the more I hurt, and the more I hurt, the more I self-medicated. Just before I had what I call my *"big breakdown,"* when I was 43, I started drinking heavily and spending time watching pornography. The thing that I detested the most in this life, sexual perversion, I was drawn to like a moth to a flame. This thing that had caused me so much pain throughout my childhood and now haunted me as an adult was the very thing that I was helping to perpetuate. I was allowing it to continue to feed on my soul. St. Paul talks about this odd twist of human nature in the following passage:

15. What I do, I do not understand. For I do not do what I want, but I do what I hate.

16. Now if I do what I do not want, I concur that the law is good.

17. So now it is no longer I who do it, but sin that dwells in me.

18. For I know that good does not dwell in me, that is, in my flesh. The willing is ready at hand, but doing the good is not.

19. For I do not do the good I want, but I do the evil I do not want.

20. Now if [I] do what I do not want, it is no longer I who do it, but sin that dwells in me.

21. So, then, I discover the principle that when I want to do right, evil is at hand.

22. For I take delight in the law of God, in my inner self, but I see in my members

23. another principle at war with the law of my mind, taking me captive to the law of sin that dwells in my members.

Romans 7:15-23

One of the things that confused me about what I was going through is that I had given my life to Christ many years before. I was deeply submersed in the Evangelical Charismatic Christian Culture and filled with the Holy Spirit. I was saved by the Blood of Christ and spoke in tongues. My wife and I were deacons of the church we attended. I was supposed to be filled with the joy of the Lord.

I was filled with anything but joy, though. I reached a point where I had honestly decided that Christianity was not real. The reason I came to this conclusion is because if Christianity was real, there was something very wrong. It would mean that God hated me and that I was not saved, destined to spend eternity in hell. In reality, I was afraid that I had somehow offended God in such a way that He had given up on me or that the whole idea of God was nothing but a fairytale.

But that was when God began to touch me in a much different way than I had ever experienced. I was not sure at first because His touch was different than I had ever experienced in the past, and it did not line up with my understanding at the time of Who God is in our lives. I would become so overwhelmed that I would have to lie down on the floor wherever I was as waves of pain surged throughout my body. It was un-controllable. I can remember being afraid that it would happen when I was in public. During that time is when I wrote the first paragraph of this chapter. It was when I learned how much God really loves me. God loves me so much that He was not going to allow me to continue to stuff any more of my pain. He was not concerned about disrupting my life. The only thing that He was concerned about was getting me well no matter how much it hurt. I think of it like going through chemotherapy. He would administer the healing touch of His Holy Spirit knowing that it was going to be excruciatingly painful. He would not take away the pain that He knew was some-how necessary, but He was right by my side rub-bing my back comforting me during the process.

The faith tradition in which I was immersed at that time held that to be in mental anguish was somehow a sign of weak faith. I, along with others within my church, would meditate on phrases like the *"joy of the Lord is our strength"* (Nehemiah 8:10) and *"standing on the Word of God"* - both good things to do, but in their proper time and place. If someone expressed the fact that they were hurt or upset about something, they would be brought to the front of the church and were prayed over—again, not a bad thing but in the right spirit at the right time. Prayer would continue until the person being prayed for either broke out in laughter or fell onto the floor, as they called it, *"in the Spirit."* If one of the two of those things did not happen, it would be said of that person being prayed for, his or her heart was hard and that the individual was unwilling to receive.

During this time of healing, through a series of events that are nothing short of divine, I joined the Catholic Church. A story I will save for a different time. While I was going through R.C.I.A. (Rite of Christian Initiation for Adults), I sought the counsel of our Pastor. God, having a great sense of humor, led me to a Catholic Church overseen by a very charismatic Franciscan Priest. This man would lay hands on me and pray on many occasions, but in a much different spirit than I had experienced in the Protestant Charismatic movement. During one of our meetings, something happened that I will never forget. I was beginning to weep, and this Pastor leaned over, looked at me, and asked me what I was feeling. This may seem like a small thing to some, but to me, it was life-changing. Sure, I had had other people ask my how I was doing, typically as something people say in passing, but when this man asked me, I had an overwhelming sense that he actually cared how I was feeling. I will never forget my reaction. I just looked at him for a few moments and repeated the question, *"How do I feel?"* I was overwhelmed and continued, *"Holy shit, how do I feel? What does that have to do with any of this?"* He did not get offended or change his tone. Instead, without missing a beat, he asked me again, *"Yeah, what are you feeling?"* The question was so *"other than"* anything that I was used to from a pastor or even from another human being. At this point in our meeting, I was expecting to be sitting in front of an open Bible and listening to the pastor read scripture verses that would remind me that God had everything under control and that my being upset was being counterproductive and displayed a lack of faith. Now the tears started to flow as I began to process the question. I had no idea how to answer, but somehow in that moment God became a person to me. I had known that God loved me and had often felt His love in a very tangible way throughout my salvation experience, but this was something very different. This man of God never opened his Bible. He was just truly concerned about how I was feeling, and it was amazing. It preached the love of God to me more than a thousand sermons ever could.

During this time, I learned of rooms in my heart that I never knew existed. For several months before this encounter with God, through our Pastor, I had wept daily, and often. The best way I can describe it is that it was as if I was completely filled with tears and that if I tilted my head just slightly, they would come running out. I would be out in public, at a restaurant, or at a store and people would give me some odd looks. I even had someone ask me if I had something wrong with me because I was continuously drying my eyes. Even when I was not thinking about anything to be upset about, tears would be running from my eyes. Now the weeping was accompanied by episodes of uncontrollable sobbing and at times seemingly unprovoked. I had started to wonder if I was losing my mind. I can remember waking myself from a sound sleep just sobbing.

At that time, I was seeing a therapist for sexual abuse survivors. She had given me several books full of writing from other abuse victims. It was like reading my own mail. The similarities to my emotional turmoil and coping mechanisms that these people developed were uncanny. It was almost like what I think it would feel like to find out you had a twin whom you never knew existed. It was very comforting to find out that I wasn't going crazy, or if I was, that I was going crazy for good reason.

It was after reading these stories of other abuse victims that I realized that my first memories of being molested were not the memories of the first time that I had been molested. After reading about the behavior of children who were molested as toddlers, I realized that I had displayed the same behavior. Like I said, it was like reading my own mail. I confronted my mother with what I had learned and asked her what had happened. She at first tried to continue to hide the event that has forever changed my life, but after continuing to press in, she told me what happened. I could see by the look in her eyes that the memories were coming back to her like they had just happened the day before.

I have absolutely no memory of the event, but I most definitely carry the scars. This new revelation was a game changer. At least now I had some idea of why I behaved the way I did. When most people think of Post Traumatic Stress Disorder, they think of it as something that soldiers return with from war. Post Traumatic Stress Disorder, or as it is also known as, PTSD, is a disorder that occurs as a result of a person's being exposed to a traumatic event that completely overwhelms the emotions to the point of despair. I have lived with this pain for over 48-years, and for 43 of those years, I had no idea what was happening. I have lived with anxiety and the sometimes-overwhelming fear that something is terribly wrong for no apparent reason for most of my life. I was constantly on the search for something to stop the feeling of impending doom. I have tried many prescribed pharmaceutical drugs and often resorted to self-prescribed medication, most often in the form of alcohol.

Let me assure you of the fact that emotional pain and suffering is completely debilitating. I never in my life understood how painful emotional healing could be before I confronted my past head-on. There were times that I did not trust myself to be alone. I reached the point of despair on a few occasions that I actually thought about ending my life. This was after I had entered into therapy. Therapy was something that I had to take in small doses and for short periods of time because it sometimes caused the pain to become overwhelming. I still, seven years later, have certain triggers that will send me into a tailspin - perhaps a news story or something someone will say to me. They are like landmines that I can't see coming.

Here is the big question. What if I had died when I was 35 years old, several years before God so graciously started my healing process, as many do? There are many who die in the heat of turmoil. There are many who never deal with their pain. The filth of sin keeps our robes stained (Revelation 7:14-17) whether we committed the offense or the offense was committed against us. One of the things about sin that we so often forget in our selfish, fallen state is that it affects everyone around us. We are all in this together. Again, what if I had died? Would I have been ready to be presented by Christ as a pure and spotless bride?

Introduction

~

The belief in a place called Purgatory is one of the Catholic doctrines that kept me from entering into full fellowship with the Catholic Church long before I did in April of 2009. I just could not get my mind wrapped around a place where God would send people to suffer for their sins.

In my mind, Christ paid for my sins upon a cross one very dark day over 2,000 years ago, on a lonely hill called Calvary, outside of the city walls of Jerusalem. He took my punishment upon Himself so I would not have to burn in hell. God is Love, not some sick deity who delights in seeing people suffer! The Blood of Christ saved me. What more was there to discuss?

My view of Purgatory, to say the least, has dramatically changed since coming to understand and embrace Catholic doctrine. I have been asked time and time again, *"Why did you decide to join the Catholic Church?"* I quickly learned that most of my Protestants friends were not truly interested in learning why, nor did they offer enough time or respect to enter into a reasonable dialog. Their questions were typically rhetorical code for *"Are you out of your mind?*

You joined a cult!" For those of you who are genuinely interested in understanding why I joined the Church, this writing on Purgatory will help in illustrating one part of my journey. I hope you will take the time to join with me in further discussion.

One of my motivations for putting down my thoughts in writing is my desire to have something to pass along to my children. This is my first attempt at creating that. Most of the answers to the questions people ask me are not a 5-minute response, as many are hoping. The greatest challenge I typically face is where to start. How do I explain something that has developed in my mind only through years of studying the Scripture? How do I express over a forty-five-minute lunch what the Holy Spirit has been ministering to me for over twenty years?

Most Cradle Catholics (Catholics from birth) are catechized (taught about their faith) at a young age and continue through life very settled in their faith (Footnote 1). They typically trust in what they are taught and do not ask many questions. Conversely, as Protestants, we questioned everything. We were taught to *"be eager to present yourself as acceptable to God, a workman who causes no disgrace, imparting the word of truth without deviation" (2 Timothy 2:15).*

When a Protestant asks a question of a Catholic, he or she is looking for an answer grounded in Scripture. Scripture is the Protestant benchmark concerning the truth of God's Kingdom. Most Protestants live, eat, and breathe the Bible and consider the Bible to be their ultimate governing authority, a platform that the Catholic Church refers to as *"sola scriptura"* (Latin for – *"scripture alone"*). Catholics, on the other hand, look at the authority of the Church differently. Catholics believe that the Church is the *"pillar and foundation of truth"* as stated by the Apostle Paul in his first letter to Timothy, chapter 3, verse 15.

The difficulty herein surfaces when a Protestant asks a question of a Catholic concerning what he or she holds as a certain tenet of his or her faith. In response, a Catholic will most often give a scripted answer that has been taught by the Church.

For example, some time ago I was participating in a small Bible study group when a new convert to Catholicism expressed frustration in understanding the doctrine of Purgatory. A Cradle Catholic in the group answered with intentions of being helpful and explained that *"Purgatory is the place where we go after we die to be cleansed of our sins after the death of our physical bodies."* While this answer is not incorrect, it is, however, incomplete. Additionally, the person providing the answer did not understand the question as it was framed in the mind of the person who asked the question. It would be unrealistic to expect of him to be a mind reader, but we must keep in mind the basic differences as to the way we come to the understanding of biblical truth that, far too often, needlessly divides.

Catholics typically do not have a problem believing what the Church teaches and most often do not understand the Protestant mindset. This is great for Catholics, but if we as Catholics are ever going to communicate to our Protestant brothers and sisters with some understanding of what we believe to be true, and share the beauty of our faith, we need to begin listening to the questions in the ways that they are asked.

What Protestants hear when they receive an answer like the one above is that the person giving the answer is completely ignorant of Scripture. Walls go up, and all communication ends. These types of answers are the reason why the majority of Protestants believe that Catholics do not understand the truth of the Bible. However, this, in reality, is not even close to the truth, when the Catholic Church, as I have so happily learned, embodies the truth of the scripture.

Catholics understand the truths of the Bible through the teachings of the Church. Unfortunately, though, it is true that the majority of Catholics have a limited understanding of how and where to look in the Bible for the scriptural texts that back up those teachings, and, quite frankly, most don't feel any need to learn scripture because they trust the Church. Happily, I can report that there appears to be a movement within the Church for its parishioners to read and learn the Bible.

Fellow Catholics, the burden is ours to reach out to our Protestant brothers and sisters in love. I am not saying that they are wrong, and we are right—to endorse such a mindset is the way walls are built. We do not need to be wall builders; we need to be bridge builders. We have plenty to learn from the Protestant tradition.

Getting back to the question asked by the convert in the small group. What she was actually asking was "Please show me in scripture where God teaches about Purgatory. Please help me to understand, because if it is true, I really want to know."

Catholics, I understand that the Church is our authority when it comes to Church doctrine, but, as I have learned, the doctrine that we have been taught is grounded in biblical truth. If for no other reason, please learn how to explain our faith through the Bible out of love for our neighbors, so that when we are asked, we can give a reason for the hope that we carry so precious within our hearts (1 Peter 3: 15).

6. My people are ruined for lack of knowledge!

Hosea 4: 6

It only takes a quick Internet search for *"Purgatory"* to fill the mind with hundreds of grotesque images of the depravity of humanity. Images depicting naked, suffering, and often burning souls that have been illustrated through paintings and various other forms of disturbing artwork throughout the history of the Church.

Please do not go to the Internet to see these images. These images are nothing that we need to let into our minds, nor do they accurately depict Purgatory. Throughout Church history, there have been misguided people who have felt that creating a picture of God as a mean, nasty, and vindictive being would somehow turn people away from sin, and toward holiness.

I love the Catholic Church, but I would be remiss if I failed to acknowledge that there have been those who have planted some very misleading thoughts in the minds of the faithful that are, in fact, not Church doctrine but have, just the same, become an integral part of Her fabric. The Church is very clear in Her belief in the doctrine of Purgatory, but, unfortunately, not everything taught by Her members, leadership, or lay is official Church Doctrine.

God is the God of Love. He is truly Love, who sent His Son, Jesus, to die on a cross for our sins. Jesus paid the price for our sins that we could not pay in 10,000,000 years in a place called Purgatory.

So what is Purgatory? Purgatory is a place where we go to deal with our past sins, but not as a penalty or punishment. Purgatory is a place of healing. There is a huge difference between the penalty for sin, which the Blood of Christ covered, and the effect that sin has on our souls. Sin leaves scars and pain upon our souls, perceived by us or not, that are in need of the healing touch of Christ. When we enter into God's Throne Room in Heaven, we will be whole beings free from *"spot or wrinkle"* (Ephesians 5:27). Jesus is our healer, and He *"who began a good work in you will continue to complete it until the day of Christ Jesus"* (Philippians 1:6).

Pope John Paul II described Purgatory as a *"condition of existence"* rather than a physical place. The goal of every believer should be to grow as close as possible to the Father, not just simply to enter into Heaven. God is perfect, and Holy, and His habitation is Glory. As we move closer to Him, we become Holy as He is Holy (1 Peter 1:16 & Leviticus 20:26). In this world, we become entangled (Hebrews 12:1) in a web of sin. Our only hope of becoming freed from this web is the healing touch of our Savior (Romans 7:25).

God is most concerned with the *"condition"* of our *"existence"* (our souls). We are here on Earth for a reason. None of us is entirely sure of why we are here or the ultimate goal of our existence (1 Corinthians 13:12), but we need to understand that God loves us and that He will not stop until every one of us, who loves Him, is made whole and has reached the goal that He has for us to achieve, the most important of which is to be with Him in Eternity.

In summary, this book has two main goals.

The first is to help our Protestant brothers

and sisters gain a better understanding of Purgatory and likewise, perhaps gain a better understanding of our Catholic faith through a few of the rabbit trails that will come up throughout the book.

The second is to give our Catholic brothers and sisters the resources to better explain our faith. Protestant or Catholic, I hope you enjoy this part of our journey together.

The next two chapters cover the subjects of *"Holiness"* and the *"Nature of God."* These two subjects are foundational to understanding the need for this *"condition of existence"* called Purgatory.

Holiness

~

When we speak of Holiness, different ideas form in different people's minds. I am not sure that we shouldn't write the word in two different ways: one with a capital H and the other with a lowercase h.

First, God is Holy - capital H. He is perfect. He is an all-consuming fire (Hebrews 12:29). Moses's face, after leaving the presence of God, radiated with His Glory: "*When Aaron, then, and the other Israelites saw Moses and noticed how radiant the skin of his face had become, they were afraid to come near him*" (Exodus 34:30). Moses "*put a veil over his face*" (Exodus 34:33) when he spoke to the people of Israel following the encounter because the sight was so disturbing that they were afraid. The people understood that to be in the presence of God meant death. God had previously told Moses that "*No one shall come up with you, and let no one even be seen on any part of the mountain; even the sheep and the cattle are not to graze in front of this mountain" (Exodus 34:3).* This instruction was not because God is shy and did not want anyone around when He met with Moses; rather, this instruction was given because God is merciful and kind. Any person or creature that touched the mountain would have been consumed with the fire of God's Holiness. On the mountain, Moses was given a very special gift. He was given the grace to stand in God's Presence without dying. In Romans 3: 23, the Apostle Paul writes, "*all have sinned and are deprived of the glory of God.*" God is Holy, and His habitation is Glory, which sinful man cannot enter without first being cleansed of all unrighteousness (1 John 1:9).

The second way of writing holy, with a lower case h, should pertain to things or people who are set apart for God or, as we often refer to them, "*sanctified,*" which means the same. We have interconnected these two words, sanctified and holy, so much in our modern culture that we have watered down the understanding of what it is to be Holy. For example, when we say "*Holy Father,*" what do most people think of, Catholic and Protestant alike? Yes, of course, we think of our Father in Heaven. However, we also refer to the Pope as the/our "*Holy Father.*" I am sure that Pope Francis would be the first to agree that he is not Holy and that he goes to confession regularly to confess his sins just like the rest of us. As Catholics, we believe that his office, however, is Holy, established by Christ, with St. Peter as our first Pope.

What is the definition of Holy? The following are the definitions taken directly from the Merriam-Webster Dictionary On-Line.

1   : *exalted or worthy of complete devotion as one perfect in goodness and righteousness.*

2   : *divine <for the Lord our God is holy — Psalms 99:9(Authorized Version)>*

3   : *devoted entirely to the deity or the work of the deity <a holy temple> <holy prophets>*

4   *a* : *having a divine quality <holy love>*

b : *venerated as or as if sacred <holy scripture> <a holy relic>*

5   *—used as an intensive <this is a holy mess> <he was a holy terror when he drank — Thomas Wolfe> ; often used in combination as a mild oath <holy smoke>*

Let's take a look at St. Matthew 12:1-8:

1. At that time Jesus was going through a field of grain on the Sabbath. His disciples were hungry and began to pick the heads of grain and eat them.

2. When the Pharisees saw this, they said to him, "See, your disciples are doing what is unlawful to do on the Sabbath."

3. He said to them, "Have you not read what David did when he and his companions were hungry,

4. how he went into the house of God and ate the bread of offering, which neither he nor his companions but only the priests could lawfully eat?

5. Or have you not read in the law that on the Sabbath the priests serving in the temple violate the Sabbath and are innocent?

6. I say to you, something greater than the temple is here.

7. If you knew what this meant, 'I desire mercy, not sacrifice,' you would not have condemned these innocent men.

8. For the Son of Man is Lord of the Sabbath."

Like the Pharisees in this account, we often misunderstand what is Holy and what is set apart for God. The Pharisees in this story missed the Savior, Who is Holy because they were so wrapped up in honoring things that are not holy as being Holy. The Sabbath is *"holy"* (set apart for God) when we *"keep it as holy"* for the One Who is *"Holy."*

Another good example of this - as Catholics we observe holy days of obligation. We observe June 29th as a holy day as we remember the solemnity of the Apostles, Saints Peter, and Paul. Why is this day holy? When is it holy? It is holy only when we set it apart as holy. It is not holy to a non-believer. Why do we set it apart? Is it to worship Peter and Paul? God forbid! Of course not. It is to keep in remembrance of what the Holy One, our God, did in the lives of Peter and Paul. Everything that we set apart as being holy other than God is only holy because it is set apart for the purpose of pointing us in the direction of God. What should come to mind when we think of Peter and Paul? Two men who did not stand a chance of entering the Kingdom of God had it not been for the grace of God in their lives. Impetuous Peter and Christian-murdering Paul (who's name was Saul at the time) are loved by God and were moved by God to repent, to be saved, and become two of the most influential saints in Church history. What should we be thinking of on June 29th as we set that day apart to remember these two men? How great and Holy they are? No! I believe that these two saints would be the first to tell us that we should rather celebrate how great, and Holy God is, how much He loves us, and how faithful He was and is in the lives of these two men.

In Revelation 12:11, God says through the pen of St. John that *"They (*believers/saints*) conquered him* (the devil*) by the blood of the Lamb and by the word of their testimony; love for life did not deter them from death."* All that we as Catholics hold as holy (set apart) is part of our testimony, not to be held in such high esteem that we miss the point, which is Christ, as the Pharisees did in chapter 12 of the book of St. Matthew. They were so wrapped up in religious pride that they could not see the Christ when He was standing right in front of them.

1. Welcome anyone who is weak in faith, but not for disputes over opinions.

2. One person believes that one may eat anything, while the weak person eats only vegetables.

3. The one who eats must not despise the one who abstains, and the one who abstains must not pass judgment on the one who eats; for God has welcomed him.

4. Who are you to pass judgment on someone else's servant? Before his own master he stands or falls. And he will be upheld, for the Lord is able to make him stand.

5. [For] one person considers one day more important than another, while another person considers all days alike. Let everyone be fully persuaded in his own mind.

6. Whoever observes the day, observes it for the Lord. Also whoever eats, eats for the Lord, since he gives thanks to God; while whoever abstains, abstains for the Lord and gives thanks to God.

7. None of us lives for oneself, and no one dies for oneself.

8. For if we live, we live for the Lord, and if we die, we die for the Lord; so then, whether we live or die, we are the Lord's.

9. For this is why Christ died and came to life, that he might be Lord of both the dead and the living.

10. Why then do you judge your brother? Or you, why do you look down on your brother? For we shall all stand before the judgment seat of God

Romans 14: 1-10

Although he never uses the word *"holy,"* St. Paul touches on the subject of things that are set apart for God in Romans 14:1-10. In this particular instance, he is writing to the Church in Rome in an attempt to settle disputes between newly converted Jews and newly converted Gentiles. The Jews were offended at the Gentiles' liberty in celebrating or offering certain days to the Lord that may have originated as pagan holidays. Additionally, they were eating meat offered to idols. Paul attempts to explain that what we hold as holy, or set apart for God, is holy because we set it apart in our hearts. For example, is a holy day, holy vestment, or holy shrine holy because it is inherently so? No, they are holy when we keep them holy or set them apart for the service of God, Who is Holy. What makes the Sabbath holy? Again, our keeping of the Sabbath as holy is what makes it holy. In Exodus 20:8, God passes down The Law and commands, *"Remember the Sabbath day – keep it holy [set apart for God]."*

What does any of this have to do with Purgatory? We need to understand Holiness to understand why we need a place called Purgatory. Nothing that is unholy will be allowed in the presence of God. This includes any person. Just as Jesus explains in St. Mark 2:27 that the Sabbath is for man, so also Purgatory is for the good of man, not a place where God gets some type of sick pleasure out of tormenting suffering souls.

Yes, there is suffering in Purgatory, but not because God is punishing people. The suffering is happening because of the wages of sin (Romans 6:23), the fruit of sin being harvested in the lives of the suffering (the consequences).

I will use the events of my own life as an example of this. When I was a toddler, I was sexually abused by an uncle. I have forgiven that uncle, and I pray that God has forgiven him as well. However, that event has caused immeasurable pain in my life and in the lives of many around me as a result of my actions in dealing with the pain of that sin (the web of sin in which we are all entangled). The pain of that one incident has continuously resurfaced throughout my life. That pain is not the result of God punishing anybody; it is the natural consequence of sin. God can forgive all of the sins committed as a result of that one event, but it does not immediately take away the pain or suffering. God is our healer. God heals us through the stripes of His Son (Isaiah 53:5). Jesus took the punishment for our sins upon the cross, allowing the healing to begin, but it was not, and is not, immediate. Often the pain from sin takes longer than a lifetime to heal.

24. He himself bore our sins in his body upon

the cross, so that, free from sin, we might live for righteousness. By his wounds you have been healed.

1 Peter 2:24

The good news is that through the pain that Christ suffered on the cross we will one day be Holy as Christ is Holy (1 Peter 1:16) if we should choose His invitation, pick up our crosses, die to self daily (choosing His will over our own), and follow Him (St. Luke 9:23). With the Cross comes pain and suffering, a path with Him that will eventually lead to our deaths. This death will allow us to enter into full communion with the Father, Son, and Holy Spirit. Until that day, though, we are pilgrims in a strange land (1 Peter 2:11) to which we do not belong, working out our own salvation with fear and trembling (Philippians 2:12). Dying on a cross is a fearful and painful thing. Christ's *"sweat became like drops of blood"* (St. Luke 22:44) at the anticipation of His Holy act of love. We are no different. The pain of dying to self is excruciating.

Jesus gave Himself on the cross through love, as He is Love (1 John 4:16). His purpose in this creation story, of which we (all people) are His focal point, is to sanctify us. His desire is to unite us as Holy to Himself before His (our) Father in

Heaven. St. Paul writes in Ephesians 5:27, *"that he might present to himself the church (His Bride) in splendor, without spot or wrinkle or any such thing, that she might be holy and without blemish."* St. John describes the wedding day in Heaven between Jesus and His Bride, the Church, in Revelation 19:7-8: *"Let us rejoice and be glad and give him glory. For the wedding day of the Lamb has come, his bride has made herself ready. She was allowed to wear a bright, clean linen garment."*

In 1 Peter 1:16, the Apostle reminds us that the Lord calls us to be Holy as He is Holy. This is more than just a good idea; it is a commandment for those who follow Him (Leviticus 20:26). This commandment was part of the Old (first) Covenant, also referred to as *"The Law."* Christ came to free us from The Law, which was a covenant of rules impossible for any man to keep in our fallen state. If keeping The Law was the way of salvation, none would be saved. The Good News is that God, in His perfect, compassionate love stepped out from behind His veil of eternity and entered into our realm of time and space to save us. He gave us The Law to show us how sinful we are, and as part of His perfect plan, He rescued us from our own sinful nature through the New Covenant, the Body, and Blood of His Son, Jesus

Christ. Holiness can never be achieved by the keeping of laws and mandates. God's awesome display of power and might upon Mount Sinai was not enough to cause the Israelites to follow Him in Holiness. God shook the earth and appeared in great displays of fire and smoke, but He did not capture the human heart until He stepped out of Heaven in love and came to us in the form of a helpless child. It is by Love (God's Spirit) that the human heart is captured, not through displays of power and might (Zachariah 4:6). Likewise, we will never reach a state of Holiness by focusing on the awesome things God does on the Earth, like looking for a sign. The only way that we will ever reach Holiness is through falling helplessly and passionately in love with Jesus, the Risen Christ. The Bible is a love letter, not a book of rules and regulations.

Why does God so passionately desire for us to become Holy? The answer is very simple: nothing that is unholy can enter fully into His presence. He is Holy and desires to be in full and complete union with us. It is hard to understand why the Creator of the universe would want anything to do with me. Who am I that the God of the universe locks His gaze on me from over the balcony of Heaven with a desire for my full commitment to Him in love? We always ask the question *"Where is God?"* when the real question in this romance story is *"Where are we?"* God has given us everything, and we continue to give Him merely our leftover attention, when and if we have time.

How many of us will be Holy when we die? How many are completely clean and pure, ready to enter into the presence of God? The answer is not many of us, if any. So the big question is "Who is good enough to enter into Heaven?" Any of us who have been in church for any length of time understand that the answer is that nobody is good enough. The only way that any of us will ever enter into Heaven is through the saving grace of Jesus the Christ, through the washing of His perfect Blood.

Many Christian groups teach and believe that if someone has given his or her life to Jesus and is saved, when that person dies, he or she will be immediately ushered into the Throne Room of God to join in worship with the four and twenty Elders (Revelation 4:4). I walked with these groups for many years in complete frustration. I always wondered what was wrong with me. There was always that nagging question in the back of my mind: Does Jesus really love me? Why, if I am saved, do I still have unclean thoughts and do foolish things? Have I offended God to the point that He has rejected me? Let us be completely and painfully honest with ourselves. What is the first rule in most addiction recovery programs? The addict must admit that he or she has a problem. How many of us, if we died right now, are perfect and clean enough to enter into the presence of God?

St. Anthony of Egypt, whom many consider to be the Father of Monks, hid himself in an abandoned soldier's fort for 20 years, living the life of a hermit drawing close to Christ in an attempt to overcome his sinful nature. When St. Anthony finally left the confines of the soldier's fort, he went on to be a major influence for God within the Church. It was said of him that people were drawn to his kind spirit. St. Anthony lived to be 105 years of age. Toward the end of his life, now well established in the wisdom that is only obtainable by a long life of being in Christ, he returned to the solitude of the desert so he could spend his last days focused on God. Despite his living what many in the Church would say a very holy life, he considered himself to be sinful and clung to God for all hope (St. Anthony of Egypt and the Desert Fathers & Mothers).

So what chance do any of us have? With Jesus, we have every chance! Jesus is our healer (St. Matthew 13: 15 – St. Luke 4:18). What does the Bible say about healing in Heaven? In Revelation chapter 21, St. John describes seeing the New Jerusalem, the Holy City, coming down from Heaven. In verse 4, it says that *"He will wipe away every tear from their eyes, and there shall be no more death or mourning, wailing or pain, (for) the older has passed away."* This verse very clearly describes a time after this present age has passed away and speaks toward a future event. I understand that God is eternal and that many believe time does not apply to the eternal realm; however, God is giving St. John this revelation in terms that he and his readers can understand.

1. "Then the angel showed me the river of life giving water, sparkling like crystal, flowing from the throne of God and of the Lamb

2. down the middle of its street. On either side of the river grew the tree of life that produces fruit twelve times a year, once each month: the leaves of the trees serve as medicine for the nations.

3. Nothing accursed will be found there anymore. The throne of God and of the Lamb will be in it, and His servants will worship

Him."

Revelation 22:1-3

In the text above, St. John very plainly communicates that healing takes place in Heaven. All who enter into Heaven may not be ready to enter into the New Jerusalem. There are many who are laying on the banks of the river that flows from the Throne of God and the Lamb, being washed by its healing waters and being healed by the leaves of the trees that grow along its banks. I can picture Jesus walking along its banks, stopping to spend as much time as needed, wiping away the tears and pain of hurting suffering souls.

Jesus covers our sin with the Blood of His eternal sacrifice and washes from us the pain of this life with the water of His love (Ephesians 5:26). With His Head held high, He will then take us by the hand, walk us through the gates of the New Jerusalem, and present us, dressed in pure, clean, white linen to His Father as His Holy Bride (Ephesians 5:26).

The Nature of God

~

One of the most important aspects of our walk with God, our Father, is our perception of Who He is and what He is like. When Moses asked God, *"if I go to the Israelites and say to them, 'the God of your ancestors sent me to you,' and they ask me, 'what is his name?' what do I tell them?" (Exodus 3:13).* He answered Moses very simply: *"I Am Who I Am"* (Exodus 3:14). Then He added, *"This is what you will tell the Israelites: 'I AM has sent me to you'" (Exodus 3:14).* How do we describe God? How could we even begin to perceive Who He is within the confines of the human mind? He is Who He is.

We may never know Who He is completely, but we can certainly have some understanding of His nature by listening to and reading the accounts of the way He has treated people throughout history and the way He has treated us throughout our own lives.

What is His nature? What is He like? The way we answer these two questions will answer the question as to the way we worship or relate to God. The answer will also, more importantly, give a reason for the way we draw close to God, or instead push Him away. Do we perceive God as approachable or as a mean old tyrant whom we would not want to be anywhere near? Is He a warm, loving Father, Who loves us unconditionally, or is He a Father Who never approves of anything we do and is constantly looking for ways to punish us?

One of my favorites—and I must admit I have favorites—among the venerated saints of the Catholic Church is St. Therese of Lisieux. I have found great comfort in her writings and in the different biographical and autobiographical accounts of her life. This *"little flower"* of the Church seemed to grasp firmly, at a very young age, the human psyche and the important need to love and to be loved. God blessed her with wisdom beyond her years in what has been described as *"her little way"* (manuscript C of her autobiography). As much as I enjoy reading about this beautiful inspiration of faith, I have always wanted to know more about her mother and father, Louis and Zelie Martin, the couple who raised this child who grew to be a woman who gave her life as a Carmelite sister in such a notable way. Not only did Therese give her life to our Father in Heaven, she also had four other sisters who also joined the Carmelite order.

As a father, I have often wondered, what did Zelie and Louis do to instill such a love for our Lord within their daughters? They must have been amazing examples of God's Love in the lives of their children. It is said that Louis and his wife Zelie committed all of their time and effort toward raising their daughters. In chapter one appropriately titled *"Earliest Memories,"* of Therese's autobiography "Story of a Soul", she writes of very warm memories of her mother and father. Zelie died when Therese was just four years old, but in those four years, she created memories in her daughter's mind that gave Therese a seemingly unshakeable love towards her Father in Heaven. As a side note, Louis and Zelie Martin were recently canonized as Saints of the Catholic Church on October 18, 2015. I was very happy when I heard this news since I believe I am one of many who found inspiration in the lives of these two great examples of parenthood.

Throughout history, Purgatory has been described as a place where suffering souls are being tormented as punishment for sins they have committed in this life. Two things must be understood before we move along any further. The first is that Jesus gave His life and poured out His Blood upon a cross as payment for every sin that has ever been committed or ever will (St. John 3:16). There are no souls in Purgatory who are not in Christ. The only souls who are suffering as a punishment for sin are those who have chosen hell by rejecting Christ. Therefore, there are no souls in Purgatory being punished for past sins. We can confidently say this because the only souls who are in Purgatory are those who have been saved by the Blood of Christ. This is not to say, though, that there are no souls suffering in Purgatory. The suffering in Purgatory is intense beyond what most can understand in this life, but they are not suffering at the Hand of God; they are suffering as the result of consequences of sins they have committed and sins that have been committed against them.

Christ died once for sin (Romans 6:1-10) as a perpetual offering for the forgiveness of the sins of all of the souls who belong to the Church, His Body. To teach or even believe that God will punish those who belong to the Body of His Son, the Church, is to refute the efficacy of His precious Blood. Every time we celebrate Mass and partake in the sacrament of the Eucharist, receiving the Body and Blood of Christ, we are saying that we believe in the atoning work that Jesus Christ completed on the cross that is perpetually carried out to this day and will be carried out until the end of the age. You are forgiven—this is *"the good news of the Gospel!"*

The second thing that we must understand about Purgatory is that souls who enter into this place are not there because God has a desire to punish them for sin. God places them in Purgatory so that He can heal them from the pain of sin. Regardless of what has been taught by many throughout the age, God is not a hateful disciplinarian who is looking for reasons to punish humanity. Quite the contrary is true. He is a loving Father, Who is looking for every way to heal humanity. Why would God send His Son to save us if He wanted to punish us for our sins? The answer is simple: He would not. God is not crazy. He is not like many of the fathers who raised us by telling us that they love us while putting us down in the next breath. The perception that God is a cross disciplinarian is perfectly understandable. There are many places in scripture where it appears that God is unmercifully punishing people. We need to be careful pitting a few misunderstood sections of the text against an entire sea of passages that paint a picture of God being kind and merciful. As children, we quite often misunderstood the intentions of our parents, but once we grew in maturity and had children of our own, most of those misunderstood actions made perfect sense. How does the saying go? *"I hate it when I hear my father's words coming out of my mouth!"*

As parents, our most important role is to teach our children about God. We are to be examples of His love to our sons and daughters. Unfortunately, in our broken world, this all too often does not happen. The majority of parents started their jobs as parents with a handful of broken tools, never mind a toolbox. We live in a world of absent fathers, which leaves mothers who are completely overburdened with the task of raising children. For years, I was responsible for overseeing and hiring young men in the construction trade. As sad as it is to say, the majority of those young men grew up without a father living in their households. The number of males being raised by single women in our modern culture is astounding.

Most young men today have no idea of how to interact with a male authority figure. Respect is something that they have not learned in the true Godly sense of the word. They consider respect to be something that is earned through proving themselves as being tough enough to stay the course, which is the world's definition. They do not understand that respect is not something that is earned, but is something that we give. They have little respect for older men because they have been let down by men over and over again. Many of them have even witnessed men taking advantage of their mothers and ducking out of their lives as soon as the things get tough. Quite often, these young men will introduce themselves at job interviews by saying something like *"What's up dude"* or *"Hey man, how's it going?"* Once they are hired, the simplest of corrections on the job site could turn into a major battle. They quite often relate being corrected to being *"disrespected"* and conclude that the boss does not like them or that they are in some type of trouble. Many of them will go from job to job with a chip on their shoulder.

Quite understandably, this is the same attitude that many people have toward God. They hear God described as their Father in Heaven, but what does that mean in the mind of a young person who has watched his earthly father be anything but loving? There is nothing new about men being poor role models. Our world is broken, and as much as it pains me to admit, most men left to their own devices are not typically good examples of Godly living. I heard it once said that on every continent and among every culture that has ever existed, there is evidence of alcohol and gambling. It is natural for men and women to be competitive, fall into addictions, and to be hateful and selfish.

We learn most often by example. My two-year-old grandson, Noah, watches me at every turn. Quite often with my busy mind, I miss the subtle little signs that he is learning from me. So thank the Lord He gives us wives. He knew that they would be the only chance that most of us men have of making it through. My wife will point out to me these little signs that I so easily miss. One day I was working in the yard on a landscaping project. I stood back to examine my work with my arms crossed and my head cocked to one side deep in thought when my wife got my attention and pointed to Noah. He was standing there next to me in the same position. And when I tilted my head to the other side, he would tilt his in the same way. Children learn by example even if they do not understand that that is what they are doing. If this little guy watches me act disrespectfully to other people, what do you think he will do? And what do you think Noah will do if he watches me love and respect the people around me? It is our responsibility as men to lead the younger generation in the way they should go. We are to be followers of the su-pernatural God and not to be followers of the world. We are to keep our hearts and minds on things above (Colossians 3:2), so we can follow our loving Father's every example, just as Noah keeps his eyes on me. One day Noah might stray and follow the world for a time, but if I take the time to be an example of God's love in his life, he will have the truth to grab hold of when he gets tired of following a lie.

6. Train the young in the way they should go; even when old, they will not swerve from it.

Proverbs 22: 6

We are here on earth for a reason. The Bible says that God knew us before He formed us in the womb (Jeremiah 1: 5). He has clearly let us know that we are here for a reason. That reason is to follow Him back into grace—to follow Jesus. Something happened that caused man to fall from grace, so we live in a fallen, sinful world. We just do not know what happened. We understand that Adam and Eve fell to the temptation in the Garden of Eden, but I have the feeling that there is much more to the story. I have this feeling that one day we will wake from this world and remember the world that we came from and remember what happened—the reason we have been sent on this journey.

This feeling is not much more than an inkling. It has no deep theological foothold; it is just simply a sense that there is so much more to this journey we are on than we are told through Scripture, or that we can understand. The closer I draw to God, the more I become uncomfortable in this life. There are times when I am stopped in my tracks by what I can only describe as what feels like God intently gazing at me from over the balcony of Heaven. During these moments, I feel such an amazing, familiar comfort. It's a feeling that I somehow sense I have known for much longer than I can understand. I feel like I can almost remember something that just will not come to the forefront of my mind. It is almost like hearing an old song or going home to see your parents and the smell of the house brings back childhood memories almost all but forgotten.

When Jesus tells Nicodemus in St. John Chapter 3, that we must be *"born again,"* He also communicates something very interesting in verse 8.

8. The wind blows where it wills, and you can hear the sound it makes, but you do not know where it comes from or where it goes; so it is with everyone who is born of the Spir-

it.

I am not talking about some type of odd, new age spirituality. My point is that we know so very little about God and His Kingdom. He has given us just enough information to be able to live out the lives that He has intended for us. Our purpose in this life is to keep our eyes focused on the goal, and that goal is Jesus.

1. If then you were raised with Christ, seek what is above, where Christ is seated at the right hand of God.

2. Think of what is above, not of what is on earth.

3. For you have died, and your life is hidden with Christ in God.

4. When Christ your life appears, then you too will appear with him in glory.

Colossians 3:1-4

In the following excerpt from his poem, *"Intimations of Mortality,"* William Wordsworth reflects upon this inclination. We are here for a purpose, and the longer we are here in this place called Earth, the farther and farther we move away from God. It is like a childhood memory that slowly fades away with time - like the promise to always love a childhood friend. As life goes by, earlier promises are so easily un-kept. The drawing of the world pulls us away - college life, seeking a professional career, new relationships, etc.

"Our birth is but a sleep and a forgetting:
The Soul that rises with us, our life's Star,
Hath had elsewhere its setting,
And cometh from afar:
Not in entire forgetfulness,
And not in utter nakedness,
But trailing clouds of glory do we come
From God, who is our home:
Heaven lies about us in our infancy!
Shades of the prison-house begin to close
Upon the growing Boy,
But He beholds the light, and whence it flows,
He sees it in his joy;
The Youth, who daily farther from the east
Must travel, still is Nature's Priest,
And by the vision splendid
Is on his way attended;

At length the Man perceives it die away

And fade into the light of common day."

William Wordsworth

Intimations of Immortality

One day we will awaken from what I often refer to as this *"grand illusion"* that we call life. This life is not about this life. The questions that we should all be asking ourselves are *"Why are we here?"* and *"Do we believe that God created us?"* Very soon after I realized that I truly believed that God is real—and not only that He is real, but also that He is more than an active participant in my life—the questions changed. The questions changed from *"God, are you real?"* to *"God, what do you want from me during this life, and what am I here for?"*

What are the two greatest commandments? When a Pharisee asked Jesus which is the greatest commandment, He answered as follows:

37. He said to him 'you shall love your God, with all your heart, with all your soul, and with all your mind.

38. This is the greatest and the first commandment.

39. The second is like it: You shall love your neighbor as yourself.

40. The whole law and the prophets depend on these two commandments'.

St. Matthew 22:37-40

The formula for what God intended for us in this life, broken down into the most common denominator, is Love! God is Love (1 John 4:8), and we are to walk with God. In Genesis 5:24, the word reads, *"Enoch walked with God; and he was not, for God took him."* Enoch is one of two people written of in the Old Testament who were taken into Heaven without dying a natural death. The other is the prophet, Elijah. The event is recorded in 2 Kings 2:1-12. It is my understanding that through God's grace, that these two men achieved the purpose for this life: to be loved and to learn to love as God intends. To walk in love is to walk with God. God's love is multi-faceted. He loves us as a Father, a Mother, a Spouse, and a Friend, and in countless ways that we, His children, cannot begin to comprehend.

St. Paul writes in his letter to the church at Ephesus this very moving prayer:

14. "For this reason I kneel before the Father,

15. from whom every family in heaven and on earth is named,

16. that He may grant you in accordance with the riches of His Glory to be strengthened with power through His Spirit in the inner self,

17. and that Christ may dwell in your hearts through faith; that you, rooted and grounded in love,

18. may have the strength to comprehend with all the holy ones what is the breadth and length and height and depth,

19. and to know the love of Christ that surpasses knowledge, so that you may be filled with all the fullness of God.

20. Now to Him who is able to accomplish far more than all we ask or imagine, by the power at work within us,

21. to Him be glory in the church and in Christ Jesus to all generations, forever and ever. Amen."

Ephesians 3:14-21

As St. Paul writes above, it is very difficult, if not impossible, for the human mind to understand fully, nor can the heart fathom, the depth of God's love for His children. We must understand that there is a war taking place during every moment of every day for the hearts and minds of humanity. The enemy of our souls, who is the devil, the god of this world, seeks not just to harm us, but to kill us at every opportunity by separating us from the love of our Father. He is deceptive, and he will stop at nothing to devour our souls into hell. One of the greatest weapons of his warfare is to deceive us into believing that he is not real. St. Paul in 2 Corinthians tells us that the god of this world (who is the devil) has *"blinded the minds of unbelievers"* so that they will not see the light of God's truth. This truth is that (St. John 3:16-19 paraphrased) God is Love and that He sent His only begotten Son into the world so that *"whoever believes in him will not be condemned, but whoever does not believe has already been condemned, because he has not believed in the name of the only Son of God. And this is the verdict, that the light came into the world, but people preferred the darkness to light, because their works were evil".* The works of the flesh and the *"concern for the flesh is death, but the concern for the spirit is life and peace. For the concern of the flesh is hostility toward God; it does not submit to the law of God, nor can it; and those who are in the flesh cannot please God" (Romans 8:6-8).* Remember that St. Paul is not talking about our bodies when he is talking about our flesh. He is talking about the part of us that is carnally minded and follows the world system. Likewise, when God refers to the world as being evil, He is not talking about the literal planet, He is talking about the fallen world system of which Satan is the ruler. The flesh (not the body) is subject to the world system (not the planet) of which Satan is the ruler (its god).

As mentioned above, most of us were raised by parents who, however unintentionally, did a very poor job of being adequate examples of God's love. They bought into the world's idea of love. What is love? Is love an emotion? Is love something that is given to us or that we give to others when they are doing what we want them to do for our benefit? This is quite often the example displayed to us by our fellow human beings. Parents who tell us they love us, but as soon as we do something that they do not approve of, give us the cold shoulder. Or boyfriends, girlfriends, or spouses who punish us with silence because they don't agree with us about something trivial like where to go to dinner or what movie to see. These are examples of what is called manipulation or control, not love. In our world, for the most part, the definition of love has been interchanged with words like *"lust"* and *"like"*. How many people are actually in love with pizza? And we call having sex *"making love."* The expression *"having sex"* and *"making love"* are often used interchangeably in this fallen world - but in our hearts, we know better. Sex as God intended, is a good thing; it is an act meant by God to be shared by two married people who are in love. I am not saying that the beautiful act of making love that takes place in the marriage bed is wrong or that we should not refer to it as *"making love."* What I am saying is that we all too often pervert the definition of the phrase, something meant to be holy and good, by using it to describe two people *"hooking up"* for casual sex.

We call pictures of people having sex or of people taking their clothes off on a stage *"adult entertainment."* It is no wonder that our world has an entirely wrong definition of love or what it means to be a man or women. When I was a child, sex was everywhere. It was in magazines at our friends' houses, our parents watched talk shows that focused on sex, and it was the main focus of the music we listened to and the movies we watched. And it is still this way today. This is nothing new; lust and sexual perversion are believed by many to be the reason for the downfall of the Roman Empire.

What does any of this have to do with the nature of God? None of this changes the nature of God, but it absolutely changes the world's perception of God. As an example, many people who have been sexually abused often expect that the individuals they are being counseled by will eventually abuse them. Why? Most abusive people use kindness as a way of gaining the confidence of their victims. They quite often act as if they are trying to help the people they abuse. A predator will offer to give a child candy or to help him find his way home; a man will lavish a woman with gifts and kindness, only to become violent when things aren't going his way; and teachers will befriend students for the purpose of luring them into sexual relationships.

When an individual has a history of being treated kindly and then later abused by those previously kind people, he or she becomes accustomed to that behavior. Therefore, when a counselor is kind to an abuse victim, the victim often associates that behavior with being set up for abuse.

Many people who have been abused from a young age don't even realize that what was done to them was wrong or abusive. They grow up with the understanding that people who tell them that they love them expect something from them, and if they do not submit, there will be consequences. This may sound extreme to some, but take a really honest and hard look at the world around us. How many of our actions are truly charitable or completely out of unselfish love for another person? When is the last time someone has done something for you with completely unselfish intent? If you are fortunate enough to have had someone bless you with unselfish intent, you probably felt a little uneasy.

It is completely out of the ordinary for someone to do something for us without expecting something in return. Have you ever given a gift to someone, typically an adult, only to have that person refuse to accept your act of kindness? They most often respond with *"that's too much"* or *"I couldn't possibly accept something like this."* A small child will not typically respond in this way. A small child will accept the gift with absolutely no trepidation whatsoever. Most small children are trusting; they have not been tarnished by the world system. They believe in Santa, a fat, old fatherly figure who comes in the middle of the night, gives them gifts and asks nothing in return except that they are nice to one another.

If the God we serve is Love, which would mean that His nature is Love, we need to understand exactly what this means. What is the true meaning of love? St Paul in 1 Corinthians chapter 13 gives us great insight as to the behavior attributed to a person who is acting in love.

4. "Love is patient, love is kind. It is not jealous, [love] is not pompous, it is not inflated,

5. it is not rude, it does not seek its own interests, it is not quick-tempered, it does not brood over injury,

6. it does not rejoice over wrongdoing but rejoices with the truth.

7. It bears all things, believes all things, hopes all things, endures all things.

8. Love never fails. If there are prophecies, they will be brought to nothing; if tongues, they will cease; if knowledge, it will be brought to nothing.

9. For we know partially and we prophesy partially,

10. but when the perfect comes, the partial will pass away.

11. When I was a child, I used to talk as a child, think as a child, reason as a child; when I became a man, I put aside childish things.

12. At present we see indistinctly, as in a mirror, but then face to face. At present I know partially; then I shall know fully, as I am fully known.

14. So faith, hope, love remain, these three; but the greatest of these is love."

1 Corinthians 13:4-13

If you will take a little time with this portion of scripture - commit it to memory, make it part of your everyday thoughts - it will change your life. When you think that you love someone the way you should, go back and gauge your actions toward that person compared to these nine verses. When St. Paul wrote this passage, he was not only writing to the Church about the meaning of love, he was also writing about Jesus, Who is Love, and not only Love but also the New and Everlasting Covenant. The New Covenant is not the second half of the Bible; it is the Person of Jesus. The second half of the Bible is a record of the existence of the New Covenant and His inter-action with His people. Just as the Old Covenant Tablets were carried to the temple in an ark of gold, Jesus, the New Covenant, was carried into this world to eventually rest in the hearts of His Church by an ark made of flesh and blood, our

Holy Mother Mary. *"For we know partially and we prophesy partially, but when the perfect comes, the partial will pass away" (1 Corinthians 13:9).* This verse speaks of Jesus coming to us as the incarnate Christ and speaks toward His second coming at the end of the age. God is Love, and His every action toward us since the beginning of creation has been to lead us into a loving relationship with Himself.

I have had a few encounters with God that have absolutely changed my life. These experiences, I have no doubt, have been God reaching down from over the balcony of Heaven and literally grabbing me by the heart. One day a friend called me and asked that I pray for her husband, who was also a very close friend. He loved the Lord but was wrestling with sin, as we all do from time to time. She asked me to pray the first two chapters of Hosea over his life. At that time I am sure that I had read Hosea, but I had no memory of the text. Obviously, the first time reading Hosea did not leave a lasting impression. I believe that God will, at times, water the word of scripture with a special anointing that causes its effect to enter straight into the reader's heart. The written Word of God is divinely inspired and is anointed by the Spirit of God, and, at times, She (Footnote 2) drives it straight into our deepest parts. As I read again the words of the proph-et in Hosea, I was undone; I literally wept with a fresh understanding of God's love. This took place over 15 years ago, and as I am writing this, the emotions are returning.

Before we get into the first two chapters of Hosea, I want to take a look at Deuteronomy chapter 13, verses 1-8, which is what I consider to be a *"companion"* portion of Scripture to the first two chapters of Hosea. This section of Deu-teronomy is referring to the Old Covenant (writ-ten on tablets of stone), and the section in Hosea pertains to the New Covenant, which the Holy Spirit writes on the *"fleshy tablets of our hearts" (2 Corinthians 3:3).* Remember that the Old Covenant was designed to show how very sinful man is in his fallen state.

4. "Hear, O Israel! The LORD is our God, the LORD alone!

5. Therefore, you shall love the LORD, your God, with your whole heart, and with your whole being, and with your whole strength.

6. Take to heart these words which I com-mand you today.

7. Keep repeating them to your children. Re-cite them when you are at home and when you are away, when you lie down and when you get up.

8. Bind them on your arm as a sign and let them be as a pendant on your forehead.

9. Write them on the doorposts of your houses and on your gates.

10. When the LORD, your God, brings you into the land which he swore to your   ancestors, to Abraham, Isaac, and Jacob, that he would give you, a land with fine, large cities that you did not build

11. with houses full of goods of all sorts that you did not garner, with cisterns that you did not dig, with vineyards and olive groves that you did not plant; and when, therefore, you eat and are satisfied,

12. be careful not to forget the LORD, who brought you out of the land of Egypt, that house of slavery.

13. The LORD, your God, shall you fear; him shall you serve, and by his name shall you swear.

14. You shall not go after other gods, any of the gods of the surrounding peoples—

15. for the LORD, your God who is in your midst, is a passionate God—lest the anger of

*the LORD, your God, flare up against you
and he destroy you from upon the land.*

*16. You shall not put the LORD, your God, to
the test, as you did at Massah.*

*17. But keep the commandments of the
LORD, your God, and the decrees and the
statutes he has commanded you.*

*18. Do what is right and good in the sight of
the LORD, that it may go well with you, and
you may enter in and possess the good land
which the LORD promised on oath to your
ancestors,*

*19. driving all your enemies out of your way,
as the LORD has promised."*

Deuteronomy 6:4-19

God's intention for us has always been love
and will always be to love us and to lavish us
with goodness. Unfortunately, we are all too often blinded by the deceptions of this world and
miss out on the goodness that God has intended
for our lives. The Israelites, God's chosen people,
were often led astray by the darkness, impatiently chasing after pleasures when they could have
had the good pleasures that God intended if they
had only waited for the appropriate time. We
need to be very careful not to judge the Israelites.

We are all too often guilty of the same impatient behavior. Their behavior was natural, given that they had been led astray by the darkness, but we are being beckoned to the light by the Holy Spirit to be children of God, not of the natural world.

The children of Israel chased after lustful pleasures just as the people of this age. They worshiped *"Baals and Astartes"* in the high places and the hidden groves (Judges 2:13). They would commit perverse sexual acts with temple prostitutes and sacrifice their children in exchange for the promise of prosperity - wealth, good crops, etc. Not much different than today. Today, we chase after sexual pleasure in the name of love. When our women become pregnant, we offer up our children in abortion mills with the promise of prosperity, not wanting to be tied down with the burden and expense of raising a child.

God raised up Judges to guide the Israelites from the wickedness of the times, but as soon as a Judge would die, the people would forget that God had saved them and impatiently turn back toward worshiping the gods of the land, whom the Psalmist in Psalm 106:37 describes as demons (Baals & Astartes). In Judges 2:14, the word says that God *"delivered them (Israel) into*

the power of plunderers who despoiled them."
When the Word says that God delivers Israel into
the hands of an enemy, it is not implying that
God sent the enemy. It is implying that God has
removed His Hand of Protection. God repeatedly
saved the people of Israel from the consequences
of their sin, and they would, again and again, become impatient and return back toward the false
allure of the pagan gods.

Remember that the people of Israel at that
time lived under The Law: an eye for an eye, and
a tooth for a tooth. They lived under a set of rules
that could not, in any way, be followed by carnal
man. The Law is perfect and when followed perfectly brings life and peace with God. The problem is that no man has ever been able to follow
The Law. All men are born into sin; therefore,
The Law has become death to all mankind (Romans 7:13). Many would ask, *"Why would God,
if He loves us, set up such an unattainable set of
rules?"* God did not set up The Law as an arbi-
trary set of rules just for the sake of setting up
rules. The Law is a set of guidelines that are designed to help man see the pitfalls of sin.

Let's look at the commandment not to commit fornication - sex outside of the covenant of
marriage. What are the possible consequences of

this particular sin? The first thing that comes to mind is the soul tie that is created between a man and a woman when they intimately give themselves to one another. When a man and a woman come together in this way, they become one flesh in the spirit (St. Mark 10:8), and when that union is broken, their spirits become deeply injured—a soul tie is broken, tarnishing their hearts. When we commit the sin of fornication, we give a piece of our hearts away that belongs to another, namely our current or future spouses. Our impatient lust drags us into the selfish act of hurting other people, and we become unfaithful to our spouses, even if we have never met them. This is not to say that some people don't get away with sin.

Many people who commit fornication without being married do eventually marry. And this is also not to say that fornication is not pleasurable. Fornication can be very pleasurable. The pleasure of sin is what draws people. Other consequences of the sin of fornication are sexually transmitted diseases and unwanted pregnancy. God did not tell us not to commit fornication because He wanted to ruin all of our fun. He told us not to commit fornication because He loves us and wants the best for our lives. But unfortunately, all too often, we are way too impatient to wait for what is best in our lives. God longs for His children to grow into mature, happy people just as we do our children. What kind of Father would He be if He just let us have sex with whomever and whenever we felt the urge knowing the pain that it would most likely create in our lives without warning us of the consequences?

What would you do if you walked into a young mother's home and her three-year-old child was running around the kitchen with a knife in her hand? Most rationally minded people would be alarmed and do whatever possible to remove the knife from within reach of the child. But what if the mother of the child put the knife back into the child's hand? Again, most rationally minded people would be alarmed, think that the mother of this child was out of her mind, and most likely ask her what she was thinking. What if the mother's response was *"I do not want to burden my child with a bunch of rules, which could hinder her development as a 'free thinking' individual"?* Many people expect God to act in the manner of this young mother. Remember the deep theological insight that has come up once before in this chapter: God is not crazy!

God is a loving Father, Who is very active in the lives of His children. He has removed knives from my hand many times. He loves us and will, at times, step in when He sees us doing something to harm ourselves or another person. We just need to learn to listen. He typically speaks to us in a still small voice, which we often choose to ignore, or that we are not listening for in the midst of the chaos. Yes, He even punishes us from time to time. That's what Fathers do; they correct their children when it is needed. We need to be willing to submit. God is God and can do as He pleases, but the amazing thing about our loving Father of grace is that, most often, He will allow us to make the choice to listen and draw closer to Him, or to ignore His promptings and move further away from His embrace. I am confident that the latter breaks His Heart, but He allows us free will.

There are times when I have chosen to run through the kitchen with a knife in my hand and hurt myself or, even worse, another. This is called sin. Sin is always born out of disobedience. I have hurt others deeply because of my sinful disobedience and I truly deserve to be punished. This is the reason we need a Savior. God is just and demands justice for all of the pain that I have caused others. Jesus accepted that punish-

ment in my place. He paid the price for my disobedience. Thank you, Lord, for your amazing
love. Remember that there is a difference between the punishment for sin, which is death,
and God's rod of chastisement.

We often say that salvation is a free gift, but it
is not - it was bought with a heavy price; the
blood of Christ. This is exactly why God hates
sin. It breaks His Heart to see His children suffer
or be harmed in any way, and He corrects us not
because He hates us, but because he wants us to
learn not to harm one another. The bigger problem of sin is that it all too often causes shame or
anger that separates us from God.

Free will is an amazing gift that we all enjoy.
We all enjoy being able to make our own choices,
but the thought of free will can also be terrifying
if we really think about the awful things that
people do to one another in this life. We all too
often want to have it both ways - we expect God
to give us free will, but get angry with God when
free will goes awry, and sin manifests itself as
displayed by the very worst of humanity.

I have felt His rod of correction across my
backside many times, probably more often than I
would like to admit. Each time I did not see the
benefit in it as it was happening, but afterward, I

have most often been able to rationally reflect upon the situation and feel grateful for His loving hand of correction. In Proverbs 13:23, the writer reminds us that *"Whoever spares the rod hates the child, but whoever loves will apply discipline."* This discipline, however, is not the discipline of recompense or vengeance, but the loving discipline of course correction (2 Timothy 4:17). God will certainly punish the wicked with recompense and vengeance. His vengeance is reserved for wicked who do harm to His people (Isaiah 13:11). Please understand that God is very kind to the humble, but resists the proud heart at every turn (James 4:6). God is God; He will not be mocked (Galatians 6:7). As I am writing this, I cannot help but think of Aslan, C.S. Lewis's fictional lion that represents the Christ character in The Chronicles of Narnia. It is in the Awesome Power of God that we have peace.

"Wrong will be right, when Aslan comes in sight, At the sound of his roar, sorrows will be no more, When he bares his teeth, winter meets its death, And when he shakes his mane, we shall have spring again."

C.S. Lewis, The Lion, the Witch, and the Wardrobe

"Aslan is a lion- the Lion, the great Lion."

"Ooh" said Susan. "I'd thought he was a man. Is he-quite safe? I shall feel rather nervous about meeting a lion"..."Safe?" said Mr. Beaver..."Who said anything about safe? 'Course he isn't safe. But he's good. He's the King, I tell you."

C.S. Lewis, The Lion, the Witch, and the Wardrobe

To communicate my point in the vernacular, the God of awesome power, the King of all things, Who loves us with an unyielding love *"doesn't take crap from anyone."* You can rest assured in perfect peace in that fact, Jack. He is the ultimate peacekeeper.

Take comfort when you feel God correcting you. God corrects those whom He loves.

5. You have also forgotten the exhortation addressed to you as sons: "My son, do not disdain the discipline of the Lord or lose heart when reproved by him;

6. for whom the Lord loves, he disciplines; he scourges every son he acknowledges."

7. Endure your trials as "discipline"; God treats you as sons. For what "son" is there whom his father does not discipline?

8. If you are without discipline, in which all

have shared, you are not sons but bastards.

Hebrews 12:5

We need to learn to listen to the gentle voice of God when He disciplines us. Quite often, you will find that God has a sense of humor in our foolishness, however, difficult as it may be to see during the time of chastening. The following portion of the book of Jonah is a great example of our Lord's unending kindness. He loved and chastened Jonah even through all of his obstinate whining. He even used Jonah, *"kicking and screaming"* all the way, as an instrument of His mercy to those who had gone astray.

1. But this greatly displeased Jonah, and he became angry.

2. He prayed to the LORD, "O LORD, is this not what I said while I was still in my own country? This is why I fled at first toward Tarshish. I knew that you are a gracious and merciful God, slow to anger, abounding in kindness, repenting of punishment.

3. So now, LORD, please take my life from me; for it is better for me to die than to live."

4. But the LORD asked, "Are you right to be angry?"

5. Jonah then left the city for a place to the

east of it, where he built himself a hut and waited under it in the shade, to see what would happen to the city.

6. Then the LORD God provided a gourd plant. And when it grew up over Jonah's head, giving shade that relieved him of any discomfort, Jonah was greatly delighted with the plant.

7. But the next morning at dawn God provided a worm that attacked the plant, so that it withered.

8. And when the sun arose, God provided a scorching east wind; and the sun beat upon Jonah's head till he became faint. Then he wished for death, saying, "It is better for me to die than to live."

9. But God said to Jonah, "Do you have a right to be angry over the gourd plant?" Jonah answered, "I have a right to be angry—angry enough to die."

10. Then the LORD said, "You are concerned over the gourd plant which cost you no effort and which you did not grow; it came up in one night and in one night it perished.

11. And should I not be concerned over the great city of Nineveh, in which there are more than a hundred and twenty thousand persons who cannot know their right hand from their left, not to mention all the animals?".

Jonah 4:1-11

The Bible is a love story of a God who repeatedly forgives the sins of His children. He not only forgives them, but He is also constantly creating ways of escape from the consequences of sin. Like a mother who forgives and helps her children who never seem to stop getting into trouble, God is also very protective of His children.

We often read in the Old Testament scripture how God orders the people of Israel to kill an entire group of people. This is often misunderstood as God being mean and hateful. No, this is God being protective of the ones He loves. I have several daughters and am very protective of their well-being. They have brought home several young men over the years who were not greeted with kindness when they came to the door. Why would I be unfriendly or even hostile toward several of these young men? Because I wanted to ruin my daughters fun, as they often thought? Of course not, it was because I was fairly certain that the intentions in the hearts of these young men were not in keeping with the well-being of my daughters.

I did not physically harm any of them or pray for fire and brimstone to be cast down upon their heads, but there were a couple whom I would have paid to move to another continent. As much as it pains me to admit, on a few occasions, I gave my daughters over to the stubbornness of their hearts (Psalm 81:12) and let them date a couple of these *"fine young men."* When they came home in tears with their hearts broken, I would take them in my arms and tell them I loved them, all the while fighting back the urge to say, *"I told you so."* A little word of advice to men who are raising daughters: the words *"I told you so"* or any like phrase are not appropriate in this particular circumstance, no matter how tempted you are to say them.

The words of Jesus as recorded in the 23ʳᵈ chapter of St. Matthew reflect God's Heart towards His children. God so badly wants to protect His children from harm and gather them to Himself in love, but they are too busy chasing the false allure of the world.

> *23. "Jerusalem, Jerusalem, you who kill the prophets and stone those sent to you, how many times I yearned to gather your children together, as a hen gathers her young under her wings, but you were unwilling!"*

Once again, back off the rabbit trail.

In Deuteronomy chapter 6:4-5, God instructs His people to commit to memory that *"The LORD is our God, the LORD alone! Therefore, you shall love the LORD, your God, with your whole heart, and with your whole being, and with your whole strength."* The Jewish people have worked hard to do exactly that to this day. But somehow it just has not been enough to keep God's people committed in their hearts to their Creator. I am not judging them; I have failed right along with them. Certain groups of the Jewish people to this day during prayer and worship wear a little black box containing scripture on their foreheads and on their arms called a *"Tefillin."* Many Jewish families also still hang a *"Mezuzah"* on the doorposts of their homes. A Mezuzah is a little metal box that holds a little portion of scripture, very often Deuteronomy 6:4-19. Many Christian families have also adopted this tradition.

We have had a Mezuzah hanging from the doorpost of our home for many years. There is absolutely nothing wrong with meditating on God's Word, but without the Spirit, it is impossible for man to follow God's Word in its intended fullness. God has wanted for us to receive His Spirit from the beginning of creation, but man rejected God by choosing sin. Man walked with God in the Garden, but when tempted with the allure of being like God, Eve was deceived by the god of this world into believing that she was missing something that she needed. Man is still deceived to this very day by the same lie—the lie that is whispered in the ear of humanity by our enemy the devil. *"You can be like God!" "God is trying to keep you from the good things of this life." "You do not have to wait! Why shouldn't you have everything you desire right now?"* This has been the biggest temptation for humanity throughout the ages.

One of the oldest prayers of the Church often called *"The Jesus Prayer,"* is recited over and over by many monastics and ordinary believers alike until it becomes constant on the mind. The prayer has several forms but is most often recited as *"Lord Jesus Christ, Son of God, have mercy on me, a sinner."* Likewise, the *"Kyrie Eleison"* prayer, prayed very often toward the beginning of the Catholic Mass or often recited repeatedly in many songs, meaning *"Lord Have Mercy."* (Footnote 3) The tradition of the Jewish faith as well as with the Church is to meditate on the scripture. However, we have meditated for thousands of years and are still missing the mark.

God came to us in the form of the Man Jesus, Who is also called Emanuel, which means *"God with us."* God has always been with us, but He needed to provide a sacrifice for our sins that would be enough of a sacrifice to be worthy of the need. He asked us to give Him everything, so He stepped out of Heaven and gave us everything. The amazing thing about God's sacrifice is that He did not humiliate Himself in front of the whole world as some type of binding contract. He did not say *"if you give your life to Me, I will sacrifice Myself on the cross for you."* He gave Himself in the hope that we would come. Now He sits gazing over the balcony of Heaven waiting with great expectation for His children to come home (St. Luke 15:20). But He has not left us alone. Jesus said that He must ascend to the Father so He could send us the Holy Spirit (St. John 16:7).

The Holy Spirit is our helper. She is the one who helps us in times of trouble. She is the one who enters our hearts when we receive Jesus as our Lord and Savior. She is the part of God that man lost when Eve ate of the fruit of the Tree of the Knowledge of Good and Evil. We receive the

Holy Spirit back into our lives when we eat of the Fruit of the Tree of Life, which is Jesus. Eve, through disobedience, gave us the fruit that comes from the Tree of Knowledge of Good and Evil. Mary, through obedience, gave us the Fruit of the Tree of Life, Who is Jesus. The scripture has from the very beginning pointed to a day when God would supernaturally write His commandments in the minds and hearts of His people through His Spirit. This was the hope of the people of God. They waited for the promised Messiah, who would give them the Spirit.

Most often they did not understand what they were seeking. They, for the most part, thought of the Messiah as a King, who would lead them in victory over their enemies. They, without the Spirit, were not capable of understanding that (Who) the Messiah was, indeed, coming to lead them in victory over the enemy, but that the enemy was not flesh and blood in the form of an opposing army, but rather the enemy of their own minds and of the spiritual powers that they could not see. As St. Paul writes to us in Ephesians 6:12, *"For our struggle is not with flesh and blood but with the principalities, with the powers, with the world rulers of this present darkness, with the evil spirits in the heavens."*

We are part of a spiritual battle that we cannot possibly understand on this side of Heaven. The only hope that we have is to keep our minds and hearts firmly planted on Christ. One day we will be amazed by the answers we will receive to questions that we never even thought to ask. St. Paul also says in 1st Corinthians 13:12, *"at present we see indistinctly, as in a mirror, but then face to face. At present I know partially; then I shall know fully, as I am fully known."*

God spoke through Jeremiah of this coming time:

31. See, days are coming—oracle of the LORD—when I will make a new covenant with the house of Israel and the house of Judah.

32. It will not be like the covenant I made with their ancestors the day I took them by the hand to lead them out of the land of Egypt. They broke my covenant, though I was their master—oracle of the LORD.

33. But this is the covenant I will make with the house of Israel after those days—oracle of the LORD. I will place my law within them, and write it upon their hearts; I will be their God, and they shall be my people.

34. They will no longer teach their friends and relatives, "Know the LORD!" Everyone, from least to greatest, shall know me—oracle of the LORD—for I will forgive their iniquity and no longer remember their sin.

Jeremiah 31:31-34

St. Paul references this happening within the New Testament Church at Corinth in 1 Corinthians, which is a direct reference to the scripture written above by the Hand of God through Jeremiah.

2. You are our letter, written on our hearts, known and read by all,

3. shown to be a letter of Christ administered by us, written not in ink but by the Spirit of the living God, not on tablets of stone but on tablets that are hearts of flesh.

4. Such confidence we have through Christ toward God.

5. Not that of ourselves we are qualified to take credit for anything as coming from us; rather, our qualification comes from God,

6. who has indeed qualified us as ministers of a new covenant, not of letter but of spirit; for the letter brings death, but the Spirit gives life.

God has an amazing plan for our lives; we just need to keep our hearts and minds focused on Him.

1. If then you were raised with Christ, seek what is above, where Christ is seated at the right hand of God.

2. Think of what is above, not of what is on earth.

3. For you have died, and your life is hidden with Christ in God.

4. When Christ your life appears, then you too will appear with him in glory.

Colossians 3:1-4

When we accept Christ as our Lord and Savior, we die with Him and are born again by the Spirit, raised into new life. When we as Catholics enter into the sanctuary at church, dip our hands into the Holy Water, and make the sign of the cross over our bodies, we are signifying that we understand. The water represents our death in baptism as we enter into the Church, which prepares us to receive the Body and Blood of Christ in the Eucharist. When Christ returns for His Bride the Church, our spirits will already be with Him. We may not have a full understanding of this, but that's okay. Our being seated with Christ is one of the mysteries of Christ and His Church, and fullness of this revelation will be revealed at the end of the age. This is one of those places where we need to walk in faith. We can only walk on water if we keep our minds and hearts focused on Christ and not on the storm that rages around us (St. Matthew 14:28-30).

This brings us to the scripture in Hosea, which helps tie the Old Testament Scripture to the New. (Footnote 4)

Hosea

Chapter 1

1. The word of the LORD that came to Hosea son of Beeri, in the days of Uzziah, Jotham, Ahaz, Hezekiah, kings of Judah, and in the days of Jeroboam, son of Joash, king of Israel.

2. When the LORD began to speak with Hosea, the LORD said to Hosea: Go, get for yourself a woman of prostitution and children of prostitution, for the land prostitutes itself, turning away from the LORD.

3. So he went and took Gomer, daughter of Diblaim; and she conceived and bore him a son.

4. Then the LORD said to him: Give him the name "Jezreel," for in a little while I will punish the house of Jehu for the bloodshed at Jezreel and bring to an end the kingdom of the house of Israel;

5. on that day I will break the bow of Israel in the valley of Jezreel.

6. She conceived again and bore a daughter. The LORD said to him: Give her the name "Not-Pitied," for I will no longer feel pity for the house of Israel: rather, I will utterly abhor them.

7. Yet for the house of Judah I will feel pity; I will save them by the LORD, their God; but I will not save them by bow or sword, by warfare, by horses or horsemen.

8. After she weaned Not-Pitied, she conceived and bore a son.

9. Then the LORD said: Give him the name "Not-My-People," for you are not my people, and I am not "I am" for you.

Chapter 2

1. The number of the Israelites will be like the sand of the sea, which can be neither measured nor counted. Instead of being told, "You are Not-My-People," They will be called,

———

"Children of the living God."

2. Then the people of Judah and of Israel will gather together; They will appoint for themselves one head and rise up from the land; great indeed shall be the day of Jezreel!

3. Say to your brothers, "My People," and to your sisters, "Pitied."

4. Accuse your mother, accuse! for she is not my wife, and I am not her husband. Let her remove her prostitution from her face, her adultery from between her breasts,

5. Or I will strip her naked, leaving her as on the day of her birth; I will make her like the wilderness, make her like an arid land, and let her die of thirst.

6. I will have no pity on her children, for they are children of prostitution.

7. Yes, their mother has prostituted herself; she who conceived them has acted shamefully. For she said, "I will go after my lovers, who give me my bread and my water, my wool and my flax, my oil and my drink."

8. Therefore, I will hedge in her way with thorns and erect a wall against her, so that she cannot find her paths.

9. If she runs after her lovers, she will not

overtake them; if she seeks them she will not find them. Then she will say, "I will go back to my first husband, for I was better off then than now."

10. She did not know that it was I who gave her the grain, the wine, and the oil, I who lavished upon her silver, and gold, which they used for Baal,

11. Therefore I will take back my grain in its time, and my wine in its season; I will snatch away my wool and my flax, which were to cover her nakedness.

12. Now I will lay bare her shame in full view of her lovers, and no one can deliver her out of my hand.

13. I will put an end to all her joy, her festivals, her new moons, her sabbaths— all her seasonal feasts.

14. I will lay waste her vines and fig trees, of which she said, "These are the fees my lovers have given me"; I will turn them into rank growth and wild animals shall devour them.

15. I will punish her for the days of the Baals, for whom she burnt incense, When she decked herself out with her rings and her jewelry, and went after her lovers—but me she forgot—oracle of the LORD.

16. Therefore, I will allure her now; I will lead her into the wilderness and speak persuasively to her.

17. Then I will give her the vineyards she had, and the valley of Achor as a door of hope. There she will respond as in the days of her youth, as on the day when she came up from the land of Egypt.

18. On that day—oracle of the LORD—You shall call me "My husband," and you shall never again call me "My baal."

19. I will remove from her mouth the names of the Baals; they shall no longer be mentioned by their name.

20. I will make a covenant for them on that day, with the wild animals, with the birds of the air, and with the things that crawl on the ground. Bow and sword and warfare I will destroy from the land, and I will give them rest in safety.

21. I will betroth you to me forever: I will betroth you to me with justice and with judgment, with loyalty and with compassion;

22. I will betroth you to me with fidelity, and you shall know the LORD.

23. On that day I will respond—oracle of the

LORD—I will respond to the heavens, and they will respond to the earth;

24. The earth will respond to the grain, and wine, and oil, and these will respond to Jezreel.

25. I will sow her for myself in the land, and I will have pity on Not-Pitied. I will say to Not-My-People, "You are my people," and he will say, "My God!"

Wow! You have just read a summary of all of the Old and New Testament books of the Bible. Reader's Digest has nothing on the prophet Hosea. I have spent the last 15 years of my life fixated on these two chapters, which is a blink of the eye in comparison to the span of history they represent.

Let's start by looking at what we see and can learn about the *"nature of God"* or, in other words, what He is like. The first thing that we need to understand about God is that He is not a machine or a robot. He does not operate and make decisions with an unfeeling mind. We have emotions very similar to His. Remember that God created us in His Own image and likeness (Genesis 1:26). God is deeply hurt by the selfish actions of His children as displayed in the text above. Children cannot understand what it feels like to be parents hurt by their children until they have children themselves. And God is also deeply hurt by His unfaithful lover as is also communicated in the text above. The pain of being betrayed by someone you should be able to trust is among the deepest pain that we can experience in this life—the betrayal of a parent, child, spouse, or close friend.

Our first reaction when we read these two chapters may be to look at God as crazed and jealous. Well, wouldn't you say that would be reasonable? I wouldn't say that He is being crazed, but He is definitely jealous.

5. you shall not bow down before them or serve them. For I, the LORD, your God, am a jealous God, inflicting punishment for their ancestors' wickedness on the children of those who hate me, down to the third and fourth generation;

Exodus 20:5

I would say that God is being very honest about His emotions. What would most men do if they came home and caught their wives in bed with other men? Many a cheating spouse has been shot to death after being caught in bed with another person's husband or wife. This type of behavior is called a crime of passion and quite often carries a reduced sentence. Most can sympathize.

Somehow we think that things should be different with God; that He should not be upset. Maybe we need to look at the dysfunction of our own emotions if we finished reading these two chapters and have an issue with God's behavior. We have a term for people who commit wrong acts toward others and have no feelings of guilt for the act. They are called sociopaths. The world is full of people who have absolutely no issue with being unfaithful to a spouse, friend, or child who is standing in the path of satisfying their own self-centered ways.

Our modern world has murdered more innocent children than the sociopath called Adolf Hitler did Jews. We have websites like *"Ashley Madison"* that promote extra-marital affairs; they are patronized by millions. And there are those of us who find it easier to justify our unfaithful behavior by blaming God. How often do we hear people blame their self-destructive behavior on the fact that God does not love them? God is a very convenient excuse for people to justify the behavior that emerges from our very nature, which is sin. We need to understand that the display of any good act that takes place within the confines of this fallen world is evidence of God at work.

The very first act of goodness toward man after the fall was from God. When Adam and Eve ate of the fruit of the Tree of the Knowledge of Good and Evil, He made them *"garments of skin"* (Genesis 3:22). He knew that they felt shame and had compassion on them out of His goodness. This did not change the natural consequences of their action, but God in His goodness has given us a way of escape from the consequences of that sin through the Body and Blood of His Own Son, Jesus Christ.

God is passionate, especially toward His people. In the text above He shakes His Hand in anger—more in hurt—as a husband would toward a wife that he finds in bed with another man (Hosea 2:4-15). In the midst of His anger in verse 10, He cries out with His Heart in humility (paraphrasing), *"Why? Am I not enough for you? What more could I do?"* In verses 16-25, He has compassion on her by saying, *"You have been unfaithful towards Me, My Bride, but I will remain faithful. I will rescue you, My Bride, from your affliction and draw you back toward Myself through generous acts of passionate kindness."*

We could not overemphasize God's Humility in His words toward the people of Israel in this text. His impassioned love is displayed way beyond what most people could possibly understand.

How many people would advise a friend whose spouse cheated on him or her to forgive in such a way? Remember, this woman did not just slide off and commit a quiet act of indiscretion that she was ashamed of the next morning. She was living it up, wearing her lover's jewelry and feasting at his table. She was passionately in pursuit of this adulterous love affair. God actually builds a wall between His Bride and her lover so she cannot find him and then lavishes her with goodness and speaks persuasively to her in an attempt to win back her heart.

Notice that the Father threatens to display her shamefully, naked before her lovers (Hosea 2:11-12) and punish her for her days *"of the 'Baals"* (Hosea 2: 15). This is a description of the consequences that should be associated with her behavior, but God in His seemingly endless Compassion has Mercy on her and provides a way of escape from these consequences. He is still making *"garments of skin" f*or His children (Genesis 3:21). Now He has given us His Son, to cover the shame of the world with His Blood. All that we need to do is receive our Father's amazing gift as He lovingly covers our naked, suffering souls (St. John 3:16). This is the very nature of God—His goodness!

Coming to this understanding is where I lost control of my emotions over 15 years ago. I literally began to weep when I began to come to the understanding that the God of the universe loved me in spite of all of the unfaithful, shameful acts that I had committed. He would have been perfectly just to display my ugly nakedness before my lovers, but He instead wrapped me in the garment of His love. The Holy Spirit with Her most gentle touch began to slowly infuse this truth into my heart. This type of truth is not understood with the mind, only with the heart. We could meditate on this scripture for a thousand years (Deuteronomy 6), but without the anointing of God's Spirit, it will never take hold in our lives.

Now let's take a look at the word *"Jezreel."* I cannot overemphasize what coming to the understanding of this one word has meant to me during my past 15 years of meditating upon this text. The more I meditate on the word, the simpler the definition becomes. To put it in its simplest terms, the word *"Jezreel"* is you. It represents all of us who are members of the Body of Christ. We are *"Jezreel."*

The literal translation of the word *"Jezreel"* is *"God will plant."* The Jezreel Valley is located in northern Israel in southern Galilee and is considered the breadbasket of Israel. The wheat grown in this valley has supplied Israel and much of the surrounding area with grain for thousands of years up to this day. Please take the time to study the rich history of biblical events that have taken place in this valley. Our Lord Jesus was raised by Joseph and Mary overlooking the Jezreel Valley in Nazareth, and the gathering of the armies for the Battle of Armageddon—the last gathering of the armies described in Revelation (Revelation 16:16)—will take place in this valley on the plane of Megiddo.

The list of biblical events that have taken place in this area is astounding, but we are focusing on the grain for this discussion. Jesus proclaims Himself as the *"Bread of Life"* (St. John 6:35). The word of God is full of references to harvests. Jesus in St. Matthew 9, chapter 37, tells the disciples that *"the harvest is abundant, but the labors are few,"* equating harvesting souls with farmers harvesting wheat. In Revelation chapter 14, verses 14 and 15, an Angel steps out of the temple of God and gives the command to *"one who looked like the son of man"* to use His sickle to reap because the harvest of the earth *"is fully ripe."*

We are the wheat that makes up the Body of Christ. God has planted us upon the earth for this purpose. Remember, the mystery of the Church is that we are all in Christ, *"that the Gentiles are co-heirs, members of the same Body [Christ = The Church], and co-partners in the promise in Christ Jesus through the gospel"* (Ephesians 3:6). In Hosea chapter 2, verse 23, the text says that *"[God] will respond to the heavens, and they will respond to the earth."* In the next chapter, the prophet proclaims that *"the earth will respond to the grain, and wine, and oil, and these will respond to Jezreel."*

"Grain" – The living Christ Jesus – His Body, and all those who have accepted Him as Lord and Savior.

> *26. "While they were eating, Jesus took bread, said the blessing, broke it, and giving it to his disciples said, 'Take and eat; this is my body'."*
>
> *St. Matthew 26:26*

"Wine" – The Blood of Christ.

27. "Then he took a cup, gave thanks, and gave it to them, saying, 'Drink from it, all of you,

28. for this is my blood of the covenant, which will be shed on behalf of many for the forgiveness of sins.

29. I tell you, from now on I shall not drink this fruit of the vine until the day when I drink it with you new in the kingdom of my Father'."

St. Matthew 26:27-29

"Oil" – The Anointing of the Holy Spirit. I do not think that the Apostle Matthew points out that they sang a hymn, *"and went out to the Mount of Olives"* by chance.

30. "Then, after singing a hymn, they went out to the Mount of Olives."

St. Matthew 26:30

45. "Then He opened their minds to under-stand the scriptures.

46. And He said to them, 'Thus it is written that the Messiah would suffer and rise from the dead on the third day

47. and that repentance, for the forgiveness

of sins, would be preached in his name to all the nations, beginning from Jerusalem.

48. You are witnesses of these things. And [behold] **_I Am sending the promise of my Father upon you_***; but stay in the city until you are clothed with power from on high'."*

St. Luke 24:45-49

The promised Spirit did come as described in Acts chapter 2. Once the Spirit fell upon them, the disciples acted differently; they spoke in different tongues as evidence of the infilling of the Holy Spirit. There were people who witnessed this sign who accused the disciples of being drunk. The following is the first part of the Apostle Peter's response to the crowd.

14. "Then Peter stood up with the Eleven, raised his voice, and proclaimed to them, 'You who are Jews, indeed all of you staying in Jerusalem. Let this be known to you, and listen to my words.

15. These people are not drunk, as you suppose, for it is only nine o'clock in the morning.

16. No, this is what was spoken through the prophet Joel:

17. 'It will come to pass in the last days,' God says, 'that I will pour out a portion of my spirit upon all flesh. Your sons and your daughters shall prophesy, your young men shall see visions, your old men shall dream dreams.

18. Indeed, upon my servants and my handmaids I will pour out a portion of my spirit in those days, and they shall prophesy.

19. And I will work wonders in the heavens above and signs on the earth below: blood, fire, and a cloud of smoke.

20. The sun shall be turned to darkness, and the moon to blood, before the coming of the great and splendid day of the Lord,

21. and it shall be that everyone shall be saved who calls on the name of the Lord."

Acts 2:14-21

God is beginning to write His Word on the fleshy tablets of their hearts through the indwelling of the Holy Spirit (2 Corinthians 3:3). In Deuteronomy chapter 6, God had commanded the Israelites to meditate on His Word (Jesus), so they could keep Him as a remembrance in their minds. Now the Holy Spirit is being poured out, and She will begin Her perfect work of writing God's laws within our hearts. Jesus will now dwell in the hearts of men. The longest journey known to man begins - the travel of the distance between the mind and the heart.

"These will respond to Jezreel" – The Church is born.

25. "I will sow her for myself in the land [Jezreel], and I will have pity on Not-Pitied [Israel]. I will say to Not-My-People [Israel], 'You are my people,' and <u>he</u> [Christ the Church] will say, 'My God!'"

Hosea 2:25 (3)

God has given us a way to escape from the penalty of our sin, which is death (separation from God). That is what these two chapters are about. God, through the prophet Hosea, proclaims the penalty for the sins of His people, but through His great love and compassion, God instead of imputing the consequences of their actions provides a way of escape (God draws us close). The way has always been and always will be the promised Christ. For us in the Church, that Christ is Jesus, and as for the nation of Israel, they are still looking for Him to come. Although they wait, Jesus is the Christ. God will open the eyes of Israel, His people, at the appointed time. That is His nature. He is good and has provided a way of escape for all those He loves and who love Him.

There is so much more to be gleaned from the words of the prophet in the book of Hosea. I hope that you will take the time to explore the richness of its depths. My purpose for sharing this portion of God's Word is to display God's Goodness to you in a way that you might not have considered. God is good, He always has been good, and He always will be good. *"Glory be to the Father, and to the Son, and to the Holy Spirit, as it was in the beginning, is now, and ever shall be, world without end. Amen."*

During the time when I was writing this chapter, I visited my son and daughter-in-law and their two children. God spoke to me through my granddaughter, Esther, during that visit. I was sitting on their couch, and this 3-year-old little girl, with her big round eyes, crawled up next to me, grabbed my arm, and pulled it around her. She then looked up at me and said, *"I love you, Papa."* The heavens and the earth could have melted away at that point, and all would have been well. I was undone.

I have nine grandchildren who call me Papa. I love them all with an unending love. My granddaughter, Kaylee, came into my office several years ago and saw that I did not have a nameplate on my desk. She must have gotten the idea from somewhere that if you worked in an office, you must have a title. So she took a piece of paper from the copier and folded so it would sit as a nameplate and wrote on it, in her beautiful 6-year-old handwriting, *"Papa."* I still have that nameplate on my desk, and I consider *"Papa"* to be my greatest title.

I am only Papa because we have a Papa in Heaven Who Loves us more than we could possibly imagine. The next time you think that our Father in Heaven would send you or any of His children to a place where He burns the ones who love Him with fire as a way of punishing them for their sins, try calling Him *"Papa."* I am sure that He will not mind, for that is His name—Father. Papas don't torment their children; they give their lives for their children. As Jesus assured us, He is the *"good shepherd. A good shepherd lays down his Life for the sheep" (St. John 10:11).* Jesus poured out His Blood in payment for our sins. He took our punishment upon Himself. This is the good news of the gospel. There is, however, great pain and suffering in Purgatory as a result of the consequences of our being submersed in the sin of this world. There is a huge difference between the consequences of sin and punishment for sin, though.

The fires of torment are reserved for the fallen angels who rebelled against God (2 Peter 2:4). Sadly, there will be people who likewise chose hell rather than accept Jesus as the Christ. Let us live our lives and pray in such a way that others see the love of God within us and never choose to join the fallen angels.

Joy & Suffering of Our Wounded Hearts

~

I can certainly understand the hope and belief that the Blood of Christ completely heals us, but our immediate healing is not the promise that comes with receiving Christ. The promise is that we will be saved, which equates to being forgiven for our sins. This does not mean that when we accept the saving grace of salvation that we will not one day be completely healed from the consequences of sin. We will, indeed, be completely healed from the consequences of sin, but it is an ongoing process administered by the Holy Spirit in God's perfect time. It is perfectly normal to be suffering from the consequences of sin after we are saved. As a matter of fact, I would tend to think that suffering would be a normal sign that a believer has received the Holy Spirit. Once we receive the Spirit of Life, sin and its consequences should become much more grievous to the heart of the redeemed.

14. For those who are led by the Spirit of God are children of God.

15. For you did not receive a spirit of slavery to fall back into fear, but you received a spir-

it of adoption, through which we cry, "Abba, Father!"

16. The Spirit itself bears witness with our spirit that we are children of God,

17. and if children, then heirs, heirs of God and joint heirs with Christ, if only we suffer with him so that we may also be glorified with him.

Romans 8:14-17

Christ suffered an excruciating, shameful, lonely death upon a cross for the sins of the world. The Scripture plainly teaches that we should expect to suffer with Christ as a result of sin. When I joined the Catholic Church, the focus on Christ was so very different than it was with my previous church experience. As Catholics, we definitely share in the Joy of Christ, but there is a real focus on Christ and in His suffering.

Before, as a Protestant, I did not spend much time meditating on our suffering Savior. This is why I so much enjoy the liturgical calendar of the Church. I love focusing on the love of Christ during the season of Advent when we celebrate the joyful news that God came to us in the form of a child, whose name was Emanuel (God with us). Then we follow by spending six weeks of Lent focusing on the sacrifice that Jesus made for us through His suffering. I appreciate the balance.

It is very easy to focus on one extreme or the other. In the tradition that I came out of, the focus was primarily on prosperity and joy. As I have learned, there are a few Catholics who focus on doom and gloom and suffering of humanity, but they are a small faction of the Church that seems to get some type of perverse joy out of shaking people over hell on a rotten stick. I have been around priests who seem to glow with joy in describing the sufferings of purgatory. I often wonder how a person could commit his life to the priesthood and completely miss the reason for his vocation, which is hope and not fear.

Jesus in the following scripture from the book of St. Luke gives the reasons, or evidence, of why the people of His hometown should believe that He is the Christ. This passage is a prophecy from the book of Isaiah of the coming of the Christ and of how He would be recognized. He was giving them the proof or evidence that He was the Anointed One of God, the Christ.

18. The Spirit of the Lord is upon me, because he has anointed me to bring glad tidings to the poor. He has sent me to proclaim liberty to captives and recovery of sight to the blind,

19. and to let the oppressed go free, and to proclaim a year acceptable to the Lord.

St. Luke 4:18-19

The truly sad thing about those individuals within the Church who have this image of Christ as a very stern disciplinarian is that they are missing out on the joy of Who Jesus truly came to be in our lives. God does wish for His children to be mature and disciplined, but part of the good news of the Gospel of Christ is that He disciplines in love. Many in this life drive themselves mad trying to earn God's favor. Many believe that they have somehow done something so bad that God could never forgive them. How many men have tried in utter frustration to earn the favor of their earthly fathers only to fail? Many people walk this earth longing for something from their earthly fathers that they have no idea how to give because they have never received it themselves. It's like going to your father and asking him for a hundred dollars. If his pockets are empty, he is unable to give you what you want because he doesn't have it to give. The thing that these men do not understand is that favor from our Heavenly Father is not earned; it is given freely in love. It is absolute madness to try to earn something that is unattainable through our actions. What could we possibly do to earn God's favor? The good news of the Gospel of Christ is that we have God's favor freely given to us in love. We are all given the favor of God long before we take our first breath on this planet. The God of Eternity would not send His Son, the King, to die for someone who He did not favor and love with an unyielding passion.

This year during Lent, walk the Stations of the Cross and at every station remember that the event that you are meditating on took place because the God of the Universe is madly in love with you. Watch Mel Gibson's *"The Passion of the Christ"* and then try to tell me that you do not have God's favor. The biggest rescue mission that has ever taken place in the history of humanity was and is being conducted because God loves you with unfettered passion. Hell cannot stand in His way of getting you out of this mess.

In this life, we will share in the cup of Christ's suffering (St. Matthew 20:22). It would seem that the purpose for our lives on earth is to be wounded by sin and then to be healed by Christ of that sin for the good of our souls. This may sound strange, but what happens to a child who gets everything he wants? He becomes spoiled and starts demanding everything he wants exactly when he wants it. He will pitch a fit and go to any length to get his own way. He will cry for hours, throw things around, and then take the cookie just as soon as the adult leaves the room. Sound familiar? Yes, I have just described the nature of fallen humanity. The problem is that we wound each other in our selfish demands for what we want and what we think we need.

What good could have possibly come from my being molested as a child? Please do not misunderstand what I am about to say; there is nothing good about a child being molested. I would not stop at any length to make sure that it never happens to another, but I have found some good in the aftermath, and as odd as it may sound, I am not sure that I, given the chance, would go back and change the event to keep it from happening. The events of my life have left me with the ability to be easily touched by the pain of others. Life has become very serious. It is not that I do not find great joy in life, but it has given me a very real sense of the seriousness of the message of Christ and the consequences of sin in our lives. I am not saying this to elevate myself; this is very difficult to write.

Quite often I see other people doing things that I know will only lead them into great pain and suffering and wonder why they do not see the same. Trust me, I still make plenty of bad decisions. I am saying all of this because I somehow think that the reason we are allowed to be affected by sin in the way we are is because God, when this age has passed, wants His children to have matured into people who love because they understand love and are not just a bunch of spoiled rotten brats. Please forgive my sophomoric colloquialism, but most can relate to being around a *"spoiled rotten brat"* and would agree that they would prefer not spending eternity with one.

I have a two-year-old grandson who thinks he is invincible climbing over the furniture, and I, out of love, have jumped into action and helped him out of close calls with gravity on many occasions. The problem with my intervening, though, was that he wasn't learning a thing. The only way he has learned was in the few times when I was not able to respond in time. It is during those times that he learned that gravity is a teacher with no feelings; it will grab ahold of a victim at every opportunity and without remorse.

Now when he gets into a tight spot, over his head, and about to be taught another lesson by this teacher, he gets a look of panic on his face and usually in my direction. The look is *"Papa help me,"* and, of course, I run and help because that is what papas do. He still has not learned enough from this tough teacher to keep him from getting himself into those positions, but he will as time goes by. Of course, God is always paying attention to us and does not miss the opportunities to help us because He is out of town or looking the other way. He allows us to make our own choices, something I do not have the faith to do with my grandson. Yes, I have struggled with the question of why God would allow me to be molested. Honestly, I do not claim to understand why, but I do believe that God loves me and has my best interest in mind at all times. One day when the veil is lifted, we will understand, but for now, we must walk along in this *"valley of tears"* (the Rosary) trusting in Him.

> *12. "At present we see indistinctly, as in a mirror, but then face to face. At present I know partially; then I shall know fully, as I am fully known".*
>
> 1 Corinthians 13: 12

Many have asked me why I have sought refuge within the walls of the Catholic Church during my time of healing from the pains of being sexually abused as a child. First of all, I have sought refuge in the Arms of Jesus, not specifically in the arms of the Church. My answer is typical something along the lines of *"I think it is because the Catholic Church probably has a very good understanding of the pain that child abuse can cause within a community and more specifically in the lives of Her individual members."*

> *26. If [one] part suffers, all the parts suffer with it; if one part is honored, all the parts share its joy.*
>
> 1 Corinthians 12:26

What Does The Church Say?

~

The following is directly out of the Catechism of the Catholic Church. As you will notice there is no mention of souls being tormented by fire in a pit of punishment.

III. The Final Purification, or Purgatory

1030 All who die in God's grace and friendship, but still imperfectly purified, are indeed assured of their eternal salvation; but after death they undergo purification, so as to achieve the holiness necessary to enter the joy of heaven.

1031 The Church gives the name Purgatory to this final purification of the elect, which is entirely different from the punishment of the damned. The Church formulated her doctrine of faith on Purgatory especially at the Councils of Florence and Trent. The tradition of the Church, by reference to certain texts of Scripture, speaks of a cleansing fire:

As for certain lesser faults, we must believe that, before the Final Judgment, there is a purifying fire. He who is truth says that whoever ut-

ters blasphemy against the Holy Spirit will be pardoned neither in this age nor in the age to come. From this sentence we understand that certain offenses can be forgiven in this age, but certain others in the age to come.

1032 This teaching is also based on the practice of prayer for the dead, already mentioned in Sacred Scripture: "Therefore Judas Maccabeus] made atonement for the dead, that they might be delivered from their sin." From the beginning the Church has honored the memory of the dead and offered prayers in suffrage for them, above all the Eucharistic sacrifice, so that, thus purified, they may attain the beatific vision of God. The Church also commends almsgiving, indulgences, and works of penance undertaken on behalf of the dead:

Let us help and commemorate them. If Job's sons were purified by their father's sacrifice, why would we doubt that our offerings for the dead bring them some consolation? Let us not hesitate to help those who have died and to offer our prayers for them.

~

Please understand that when the Church speaks of *"purification"* as in section 1031, She in not speaking primarily of the forgiveness of sins, She in speaking of our *"faults."* Those character traits that are deeply seated within us, of which we need to be cleansed. Do you really think that Jesus, the Shepard of our souls, is going to let us spend eternity suffering from the pain of addiction, hatred, resentment or any other affliction? When we pass away from this life, our body dies, but our spirit continues to live. We are spiritual beings living a human experience, for a time trapped in the confines of a human body. Don't be deceived, just because this body dies, does not mean that our hurts and suffering from this world also die with its passing. We are not robots whose hard drive will be rewritten when we die. You will still be you when you enter into Heaven. We will most likely be overwhelmed with joy when we look into the Eyes of Jesus, if we are saved and have believed in Him during this life, if not the experience may not be so joyful. He will then take us by the hand and present us to His Father as a bride adorned in a robe as white as snow, but He has much cleaning to do before that day.

Forgiveness of Sin

~

What if someone in Christ Jesus dies without asking for forgiveness of their sins? The Church practices the Sacrament of Confession. The Bible plainly teaches that this Sacrament is to be administered through the priests of the Church.

> *21. [Jesus] said to them again, "Peace be with you. As the Father has sent me, so I send you.*
>
> *22. And when he had said this, he breathed on them and said to them, "Receive the holy Spirit.*
>
> *23. Whose sins you forgive are forgiven them, and whose sins you retain are retained."*
>
> *St. John 20: 21-23*

Some will die without having the opportunity to have their sins absolved by a priest. I understand that this concept may sound very foreign to our Protestant brothers and sisters (Footnote 5). For anyone who is reading this who has not taken part in the Sacrament of Reconciliation, you are missing out on a life-changing experience.

There will be some sins that are forgiven after we have died. There is the one deep theological point that we must always remember: *"God is not a jerk."* God is not going to torment anyone with fire because he or she died in car crash before making it to confession. God is not looking for ways to punish us for our sins; He has created every way possible that we would be forgiven for our sins. It is as simple as the following dialog.

Sinner – *God please forgive me for my sins.*

God – *Say you're sorry, and promise not to do it again.*

Sinner – *I am sorry, and I promise not to do it again.*

God – *Okay, you are forgiven. Oh, by the way, you were forgiven before you asked because My Son Jesus paid the penalty for your sin by dying on a cross.*

Sinner – *Then why did I need to ask for forgiveness?*

God – *So I know that you are not a jerk.*

Sinner – *(Looking up at God scratching his head)*

God – *Only a jerk would hurt his brother or sister and not feel bad for what he has done. Only a jerk would look at the sacrifice that*

My Son made for all of humanity and not feel remorse for being the reason the sacrifice was necessary.

Sinner – *(Still looking up at God with a confused look)*

God – *Do you want to come home to Heaven?*

Sinner – *Yes!*

God – *There are no jerks in Heaven!*

God, please forgive me for putting words in Your Mouth. I know that God does not call us jerks; however, there are plenty of places in scripture where the inference is definitely implied. It is the simplest way I could think of to illustrate the meaning of 6,000 years of biblical history. The dialog above may seem a bit ridiculous, but it is as simple as that; God wants us to say that we are sorry and to mean it sincerely from the deepest parts of our hearts. There is something very powerful that happens within our spirits when we confess with our mouths to Jesus that we have hurt ourselves or another of His children and that we are deeply sorry for what we have done, and He says *"You are forgiven, go and sin no more."*

Wouldn't that be amazing to be on our knees

before Jesus with our hearts broken with shame over our sin and to hear Him utter the words *"You are forgiven, I absolve you from all of your sins"?* If your heart longs for that day, go to confession, because, as Catholics, we believe that that is exactly what takes place during the sacrament.

The Priest is sitting in the place of Christ. The Church calls this *"in Persona Christi,"* which is translated from Latin to mean *"in the Person of Christ."* Remember that Christ literally means *"the anointed one."* When the priest sits and receives the confession of a believer, he is anointed by God to forgive sins as the Person of Christ in Jesus. I felt completely out of my element the first time I confessed to a priest and was in no way prepared for the blessing that I received. If you doubt that Christ is present during the sacrament, you have never received the sacrament, because if you had, you would not doubt. I think that most people say that they doubt because the sacrament scares them, as it did me. The confessional is the most uncomfortable place in the Church and the best place in the Church all at the same time. This is just like God; He seems to love a good paradox!

The Fire of the Holy Spirit

~

We must always remember that God is Holy and that we must be Holy to enter into the Holy of Holies, into His Inner Sanctum, His Throne Room. This is why God hates the sin that separates us from Him. Scripture describes God as a consuming fire: *"for our God is a consuming fire" (Hebrews 12:29).* Moses encountered God in the desert speaking to him through a burning bush that continued to burn but was not consumed by the flames (Exodus 3: 1-6).

John the Baptist spoke of the Baptism of the Holy Spirit and of Fire.

> *11. "I am baptizing you with water, for repentance, but the one who is coming after me is mightier than I.*
>
> *12. I am not worthy to carry his sandals. He will baptize you with the Holy Spirit and fire. His winnowing fan is in his hand. He will clear his threshing floor and gather his wheat into his barn, but the chaff he will burn with unquenchable fire."*
>
> *St. Matthew 3:11-12*

Jesus, just before He ascends into Heaven,

tells the Apostles to go to Jerusalem and wait because He will be sending His Holy Spirit: *"And [behold] I am sending the promise of my Father upon you; but stay in the city until you are clothed with power from on high" (St. Luke 24: 29)*. When the Apostles received the Holy Spirit in the upper room, they received what appeared to be tongues of fire above their heads as a sign that they had received the Spirit of God.

God and His most Holy Spirit have been described as fire throughout biblical history. When the Church speaks through the Catechism of a *"cleansing fire,"* she is referring to the cleansing of the Holy Spirit, not of the fires associated with the torment of hell. Some will try to say that John the Baptist, in the above scripture, when he says, *"the chaff he will burn with unquenchable fire,"* that this refers to Purgatory. No, this is a reference to Hell. There will be no chaff in Heaven. Those who are in Purgatory are being gathered into the barn. The Baptism of the *"Holy Spirit and Fire"* is something altogether different from the *"unquenchable fire"* of Hell.

I often picture our journey toward God as a progressive state of purification—God being this *"All Consuming Fire"* that we are walking toward. As we walk closer to the fire the *"stuff of this world"* starts to burn away: the hurts, re-sentment, jealousy, hatred, and shame, just to name some of the *"stuff."* We stop to take breaks along the path because the heat is too much for us to handle, but as we allow this *"stuff"* to be burned away, we are able to move closer. When we reach the end of our journey, we will be standing in front of God, this *"All Consuming Fire"*, and the flames will not hurt us in any way; they will actually become our habitation, the place where we live. We will be living in Glory with God in His habitation.

It is when we move closer to God that we start feeling the pain of the *"stuff"* beginning to burn away. We are being purged of the sin and pain of this life. Purgatory is a place of purging, just like the word sounds. When I speak of Purgatory as a place, I am not speaking of a specific place. Purgatory is not a huge pit of torment as described by so many throughout history. Purgatory is a place in the heart. We often hear people say, *"I am in a good place right now in my faith"* or conversely *"He or she does not seem to be in a good place right now."* Being in the place of Purgatory is the same thing, positional in our walk with the Lord. I have also heard people say that our experience here on Earth is part of Purgatory. If we are drawing closer to God and allowing

Him to cleanse us of our hurts and faults, I would agree. Quite often as people draw closer to God, and the pain of Purgatory becomes too great, they pull back. I know I have pulled back. The danger is when we pull back for too long a period of time. Most of us know people who have pulled back never to return. They are just not going to deal with the pain. They retreat instead into the bottle, drugs, or even bad relationships.

Our Captured Hearts

~

When I was going through my *"big break-down"*, I would wake up out of a sound sleep sobbing or I would break out in tears for no apparent reason. Although we may not be aware of the pain in our earthly consciousness, pain is affecting our spirit just the same. I often wonder what people's spirits would look like if we could see past our earthly facades? Would we see the pain that sits so very close to the surface of our consciousness?

St. John of the Cross, in his poem and commentary, The Dark Night of the Soul, explains this condition of our beings in great detail. He describes the condition of our soul and spirits as being hidden within this *"Dark Night."* This is a book that I have endeavored to read at least once a year. The writer's perception of God's interaction with our soul has been a great comfort to me through my personal healing process. This work, however, is one of the most misquoted within the church. Please read the writing for yourself. You will not regret the insight and richness that it adds to your walk with our loving Father.

St. John details the steps that take place as

God heals our fallen souls and spirits during this life. This healing is very painful at times and causes much suffering; however, this suffering is not the reason St. John titles his work The Dark Night of the Soul. When he refers to the *"Dark Night"* or *"Dark Nights of purgation,"* he is communicating a state or states of healing in which God places us during this life. The inference is that during this life God has separated our consciousness from being aware of the movements of God as He interacts with our soul and spirit. St. John of the Cross is not describing a really bad depressing period of time in one's life, although many of these periods of emotion are inevitable during this Dark Night. Our consciousness is separated into darkness from our soul or spirit, hidden from our understanding, as it is being ministered to by God in His light.

1. "If then you were raised with Christ, seek what is above, where Christ is seated at the right hand of God.

2. Think of what is above, not of what is on earth.

3. For you have died, and your life is hidden with Christ in God.

4. When Christ your life appears, then you too will appear with him in glory."

St. John breaks his writing into two parts: the first being God's dealing with our senses, or the purgation of the sensual part of man, and the second dealing with the spiritual part of our being - spiritual purgation.

The first two stanzas refer to the joy of having gone through both types of purgation, both sensual and spiritual. The poem is a reflection told by one who has gone through the purgation (purifying) of God. Kind of like a bodybuilder talking about the pain involved in working out at the gym while showing off his huge muscles as proof that the pain is well worth the results.

1. On a dark night, kindled in love with yearnings – oh, happy chance – I went forth without being observed, My house being now at rest.

2. In darkness and secure, by the secret ladder, disguised – oh, happy chance – In darkness and in concealment, My house being now at rest.

My purpose for this discussion is not to go through the poem line-by-line, however tempting. I want to communicate the joy that the author associates with this Dark Night. Yes, there will be great suffering during times of Purgatory, but the soul who embraces God's healing touch in this life will be filled with unspeakable joy and peace.

St. John, in the first half of the poem, is talking about the Lord purging us of our reliance on emotions or sensual gratification. I wish I had read St. John's words when I first became a Christian; they could have helped me to avoid years of confusion. When we first give our lives over to God and ask Him to make us clean, we do not understand the suffering that will be involved in this process. Let's face the truth: when most of us surrender to God, we are at a very low point in our lives and are looking for a change - something to give our lives purpose and hope. I know that was my story. I was headed nowhere fast, and everywhere I turned led me into deeper despair and frustration.

When we first make the motion of giving our lives over to Christ, He reaches through the veil and touches our emotions. It is like the classic first kiss in a movie. The two lovers move closer to one another awkwardly. One moves a little and then the other until that moment when their lips meet and the question they have both been asking themselves—Does the other like me as much as I like him/her? - is answered. Yes, it is perfectly acceptable to picture yourself kissing Jesus romantically. He is our Bridegroom. Most brides long to be kissed by their grooms. Please do not be confused, however. We are created for union with God, but it is not sexual; it is spiritual union. On this earth, all things are a foreshadowing of something much better in our spiritual dwelling place with Christ. The kiss needs to be thought of from a woman's perspective as leading to romance, not a physical encounter. Most men may have a difficult time with this analogy.

St. John of the Cross describes this nurturing as a child being nurtured at the breast by its *"loving mother. Who warms it with the heat of her bosom and nurtures it with sweet milk and soft, pleasant food, and carries it and caresses it in her arms" (Chapter I).* When we begin this walk with our loving Father, He touches our emotions with the sweetness of His Spirit. He comforts us with His tangible presence. I can remember a time early on in my walk with the Lord when I could physically feel Him around me as I often described it in an attempt to relate the unrelatable, like a being wrapped in a warm blanket.

Then it happened: the blanket was gone. One

day I could not feel it any longer. I can very vividly remember when it happened. I searched everywhere for the blanket that I had lost; I prayed harder and begged for God to return to me. The thing that I did not understand, though, was that God had not left me; He was right by my side the entire time. He was doing what He knew was necessary for me to grow spiritually so that one day I could have the relationship with Him for which I was created - a relationship that is built on mature love, not the selfish love of a child. In the words of St. John of the Cross, *"as the child grows bigger, the mother gradually ceases caressing it, and hiding her tender love, puts bitter aloes upon her sweet breast, sets down the child from her arms and makes it walk upon its feet, so that it may lose the habits of a child and betake itself to a more important and substantial occupations"* (Chapter 1).

The same description of God's wooing, or drawing, can be found in Sacred Scripture. The scenario is described differently, but the encounter is just the same. The writer of the Song of Songs, in the first two chapters, describes a bridegroom wooing his bride with romantic love. She falls hopelessly in love with him and wants nothing more than to lie in her bed and have her lover enter her chambers and lavish her with the romantic love of courtship. She has become spoiled with his presence (as was His intention), and when he asks her to rise and to leave her chambers, she is reluctant and will not go.

10. My lover speaks and says to me, "Arise, my friend, my beautiful one, and come!

11. For see, the winter is past, the rains are over and gone."

Song of Songs 2:10-11

At the beginning of chapter 3, the writer describes the scene when the bride realizes that the bridegroom is way overdue for his return. It is this absence of his presence that motivates her to arise from her bed, leave the comfort of her chambers, and go searching for her greatest desire.

1. On my bed at night I sought him whom my soul loves — I sought him but I did not find him.

2. "Let me rise then and go about the city through the streets and squares; Let me seek him whom my soul loves." I sought him but I did not find him.

3. The watchmen found me, as they made their rounds in the city: "'Him whom my soul loves—have you seen him?"

Our loving Lord knows exactly how to touch us in a way that will draw us close. He also knows, in His perfect wisdom, when we are ready to be drawn. We are born into a world of senses and sensual desires. The sensual desires as experienced by Adam and Eve in the Garden were proper and good as intended by our Creator. However, as most have grown up hearing, Adam and Eve were deceived by the serpent and the sensual pleasures that God intended for man to enjoy were perverted.

St. John describes the three enemies of our spirits to be the devil, the world, and the flesh. Once man was deceived into eating of the forbidden tree, his innocence was gone, therefore giving him knowledge of good and evil and removing his ability to enjoy the sensual pleasures of this world without corruption. Without being led by the Holy Spirit, sensual desire typically leads to addiction, perversion, and every unseemly behavior known to man. History has proven this to be an absolute truth over and over again. As goes the old adage, *"What is the definition of insanity? Continuing to do the same thing over again and expect different results."*

As the Lord begins drawing us close, He

touches our senses; He provokes the sensual desires that we were created to enjoy. Who better
to know how to woo us into perfect love than the
One Who is Love? However, our Lord also knows
that in our fallen nature we will be hindered
from growing spiritually in this state of sensual
bliss. Like the bride in the Song of Songs, we will
lie in our beds in a state of perpetual sloth, ad-
dicted to the sensual touches of her lover, con-
tributing nothing to the relationship. In other
words, she will become nothing more than a
"spoiled rotten brat."

Once the Lord has fully captured the heart of
His beloved, He will begin drawing her toward
spiritual union with Him. This transition into
spiritual maturity is painful and not without
much suffering. St. John calls this process *"aridi-
ties"* when the Lord removes his touch, for a season for the purpose of drawing His lover toward
spiritual union. The Lord knows that His bride
must be completely immersed in His love and be
accustomed to His touch or there is a real danger
of her returning to the sensual pleasures of the
world once He withdraws from her senses. As we
draw closer to God, the fire of His Glory begins
to purge us free from the sensual desires that
keep us drawn to this world. The bride has become accustomed to her lover's touch, and in her

pain, she will undoubtedly reach for the comforts that she once found in the world, but after experiencing the sweetness of perfect love, she will never again be satisfied with the false saccharine sweetness of the world, the enemy of her spirit.

In chapter 20 of Jeremiah, the profit utters his absolute frustration with God for capturing his heart in this way. Jeremiah, during the Babylonian captivity/exile, spoke as God's mouthpiece against the pagan practices of worship that were being practiced by the children of Israel. Jeremiah started his office as a prophet in the 13th year of Josiah, King of Judah, who started revival among his people in an attempt to draw their hearts back toward their God. Josiah was killed by Neco, king of Egypt, during a battle on the plain of Megiddo (in the Jezreel Valley). Neco then set up Josiah's son, Jehoiakim, to be King during the Egyptian captivity. In the year 597 b.c., Nebuchadnezzar, king of Babylon, destroyed Jerusalem and led its people into exile.

This was not a very comfortable time to be a prophet of God, especially one speaking against the pagan practices of the strongest empire on Earth that have just destroyed and led your people into captivity. Jeremiah was not making friends; on the contrary, he was on the fast track for getting himself killed. He was in direct opposition to the King of Judah and the Chief Priest, Pashhur, who were more worried about remaining in power and not losing their lives than honoring their God.

Jeremiah did not feel this way, however. His only concern was being faithful to the Lord of Israel. God had captured his heart in love in such a way that he was unable and unwilling to escape its grip, even at the threat of incomprehensible persecution and pain. He had been imprisoned by a love with bonds that are stronger than death (Song of Solomon 8:6). He had just been released from the stocks and God gave him words to speak against the High Priest, Pashhur, the one who ordered his arrest. This is a love of which most have no understanding. Jeremiah spoke the words God placed in his heart knowing that he would undoubtedly be beaten and imprisoned, if not killed, for his actions.

7. You seduced me, LORD, and I let myself be seduced; you were too strong for me, and you prevailed. All day long I am an object of laughter; everyone mocks me.

8. Whenever I speak, I must cry out, violence and outrage I proclaim; The word of the LORD has brought me reproach and deri-

sion all day long.

9. I say I will not mention him, I will no longer speak in his name. But then it is as if fire is burning in my heart, imprisoned in my bones; I grow weary holding back, I cannot!

10. Yes, I hear the whisperings of many: "Terror on every side! Denounce! let us denounce him!" All those who were my friends are on the watch for any misstep of mine. "Perhaps he can be tricked; then we will prevail, and take our revenge on him."

11. But the LORD is with me, like a mighty champion: my persecutors will stumble, they will not prevail. In their failure they will be put to utter shame, to lasting, unforgettable confusion.

12. LORD of hosts, you test the just, you see mind and heart, Let me see the vengeance you take on them, for to you I have entrusted my cause.

13. Sing to the LORD, praise the LORD, For he has rescued the life of the poor from the power of the evildoers!

14. Cursed be the day on which I was born! May the day my mother gave me birth never be blessed!

15. Cursed be the one who brought the news to my father, "A child, a son, has been born to you!" filling him with great joy.

16. Let that man be like the cities which the LORD relentlessly overthrew; Let him hear war cries in the morning, battle alarms at noonday,

17. because he did not kill me in the womb! Then my mother would have been my grave, her womb confining me forever.

18 Why did I come forth from the womb, to see sorrow and pain, to end my days in shame?

Jeremiah 20: 7-18

Jeremiah cries out to God in frustration and anger at the position in which He has placed him. He does not want to speak against Pashhur, the Chief Priest, knowing the pain and suffering that will rain down upon him. He has reached such a point of despair that he accuses the Lord of tricking him. He says to himself that he will not speak for the Lord any longer; he will not even speak His name (vs. 9). But then he is gripped by God's love (vs. 11) and remembers Who is the stronger in this fight. He immediately starts praising the Lord with a song at the thought of his Champion (vs. 13). Now that he has entered the courts of Heaven within his heart (Psalm 100), his focus turns from himself to God and His people. Now he cries out that it would be better for him not to have been born than to see the apostasy of his Judah. He even curses the man who brought the news of his conception to his father (vs. 14-18).

I wonder if the words above were running through the mind of the prophet just before he spoke to Pashhur, the Chief Priest. Is he giving us insight into his thoughts? Did he actually start singing praises to God just before he spoke?

What happened? How did Jeremiah go from utter despair to praising God, to lamenting the sins of his people in just a few minutes? Jeremiah gives us the answer in verse 9: *"but then it is as if fire is burning in my heart, imprisoned in my bones; I grow weary holding back, I cannot!"* The prophet feels the touch of God; he hears a familiar voice in his spirit. Remember, Jesus said that His sheep know His voice. Jeremiah knew Jesus and spoke of the days of the New Covenant when the anointing of the Holy Spirit would be poured out on all who would receive (Jeremiah 31:31-34). He felt the fire of the Holy Spirit come upon him burning in his bones like an old friend comforting him in his time of need. Remember that St. Paul describes our God as a consuming fire in Hebrews 12:29. Look at what Jesus tells His disciples when He warns them about the days to come when they will be chastised for His name's sake:

16. Behold, I am sending you like sheep in the midst of wolves; so be shrewd as serpents and simple as doves.

17. But beware of people, for they will hand you over to courts and scourge you in their synagogues,

18. and you will be led before governors and kings for my sake as a witness before them and the pagans.

19. When they hand you over, do not worry about how you are to speak or what you are to say. You will be given at that moment what you are to say.

20. For it will not be you who speak but the Spirit of your Father speaking through you.

21. Brother will hand over brother to death, and the father his child; children will rise up against parents and have them put to death.

22. You will be hated by all because of my name, but whoever endures to the end will be saved.

Sound familiar! I wonder if Jeremiah had been there in body, if he would have been biting his tongue wanting to say, *"don't worry about whether or not you will hear His voice at the right time. You will hear Him loud and clear, and sometimes you will hear His voice when you wish you hadn't, and I have the scars to prove it."* Once again, I am using borderline inappropriate humor to illustrate a point.

St. Peter, the one who denied Jesus three times in complete despair during the night of Jesus' arrest, once filled with the Holy Spirit, spoke with boldness with absolutely no concern for his life. In the upper room, the Holy Spirit came upon the apostles *"like a strong driving wind, and it filled the entire house in which they were. Then appeared to them tongues as of fire, which parted and came to rest on each one of them"* (Acts 2:2-3). The believers, filled with this fire of the Holy Spirit, walked with boldness, the likes of which they had never experienced before. Once you know the Father's touch (the Holy Spirit), you will never be the same.

Where else have we encountered this series of events in Scripture: first despair, secondly the infilling of the Holy Spirit, and finally boldness?

Yes, in the death, burial, and resurrection of our Lord. Let's take a look at the scripture:

45. From noon onward, darkness came over the whole land until three in the afternoon.

46. And about three o'clock Jesus cried out in a loud voice, "Eli, Eli, lema sabachthani?" which means, "My God, my God, why have you forsaken me?"

St. Matthew 27:45-46

Jesus cried out in utter agony and despair. I have heard this moment described in many ways—that God removed his gaze from Jesus or that He removed His Hand for a moment. However we choose to relate to the event, we must understand that Jesus died at that moment. He died before His physical Heart stopped beating. Being separated from God is the death of which we need to be concerned. God's removing of His Spirit from Jesus is the reason for His earthly ministry. Jesus came to suffer the penalty for our sins upon the cross. The penalty for our sins is separation from God, not physical death.

The physical suffering that Jesus suffered on Calvary should touch us who love Him deeply, but His physical death is not, by any means, the greatest portion of His suffering. He took the suffering of all of the sins that have ever been committed and that ever will be committed upon Himself. He not only paid the price for our sins; He also felt all at once, all of the shame and suffering of every person who has ever walked the earth or ever will:

4. Yet it was our pain that he bore, our sufferings he endured. We thought of him as stricken, 'struck down by God and afflicted,

5. But he was pierced for our sins, crushed for our iniquity. He bore the punishment that makes us whole, By his wounds we were healed.

Isaiah 53: 4-5

The pain and suffering He experienced during His passion (His betrayal, scourging, and crucifixion) should be considered with all sobriety deeply within our hearts, for the penalty for our sin is spiritual separation from God. Our salvation from that separation is by His physical death. Put more plainly, the penalty for sin is our spirit being separated from God, not the death of our bodies, but we are saved through the death, burial, and resurrection of the physical Body of Christ. Without the Blood of Christ, there is no salvation.

Let's see what David the Psalmist wrote about the Crucifixion approximately 1,000 years before:

1. For the leader; according to "The deer of the dawn." A psalm of David.

2. My God, my God, why have you abandoned me? Why so far from my call for help, from my cries of anguish?

3. My God, I call by day, but you do not answer; by night, but I have no relief.

4. Yet you are enthroned as the Holy One; you are the glory of Israel.

5. In you our fathers trusted; they trusted and you rescued them.

6. To you they cried out and they escaped; In you they trusted and were not disappointed.

7. But I am a worm, not a man, scorned by men, despised by the people.

8. All who see me mock me; they curl their lips and jeer; they shake their heads at me:

9. "He relied on the LORD—let him deliver him; if he loves him, let him rescue him."

10. For you drew me forth from the womb, made me safe at my mother's breasts.

11. Upon you I was thrust from the womb;

since my mother bore me you are my God.

12. Do not stay far from me, for trouble is near, and there is no one to help.

13. Many bulls surround me; fierce bulls of Bashan encircle me.

14. They open their mouths against me, lions that rend and roar.

15. Like water my life drains away; all my bones are disjointed. My heart has become like wax, it melts away within me.

16. As dry as a potsherd is my throat; my tongue cleaves to my palate; you lay me in the dust of death.

17. Dogs surround me; a pack of evildoers closes in on me. They have pierced my hands and my feet

18. I can count all my bones. They stare at me and gloat;

19. they divide my garments among them; for my clothing they cast lots.

20. But you, LORD, do not stay far off; my strength, come quickly to help me.

21. Deliver my soul from the sword, my life from the grip of the dog.

22. Save me from the lion's mouth, my poor life from the horns of wild bulls.

23. Then I will proclaim your name to my brethren; in the assembly I will praise you:

24. "You who fear the LORD, give praise! All descendants of Jacob, give honor; show reverence, all descendants of Israel!

25. For he has not spurned or disdained the misery of this poor wretch, Did not turn away from me, but heard me when I cried out.

26. I will offer praise in the great assembly; my vows I will fulfill before those who fear him.

27. The poor will eat their fill; those who seek the LORD will offer praise. May your hearts enjoy life forever!"

28. All the ends of the earth will remember and turn to the LORD; All the families of nations

will bow low before him.

29. For kingship belongs to the LORD, the ruler over the nations.

30. All who sleep in the earth will bow low before God; All who have gone down into the dust will kneel in homage.

31. And I will live for the LORD; my descendants will serve you.

32. The generation to come will be told of the Lord, that they may proclaim to a people yet unborn the deliverance you have brought.

Psalm 22

In verse 2, David describes the despair felt by Our Savior, in verse 23, He begins to praise God the Father, and in verse 27, our Lord begins His ministry as the Risen Savior. Jesus did fall into despair *("Eli, Eli, lema sabachthani")*; He was filled with the Holy Spirit as the First Born raised from the dead, King of Kings and Lord of Lords. He has spoken through the Holy Spirit and His Church, and the devil, the world, and the flesh (Dark knight of the Soul, Book 1, Chapter 13) have been at war with His Kingdom since. He knew it was going to happen long before He spoke His first word.

Our Suffering Savior

~

Jesus suffered greatly for the sins of the world. Let's look at the ways in which He suffered. The following is not a list as regarding importance or order in which we should work toward suffering; it is simply a way of identification. I am not saying that we should work toward suffering; if we keep our hearts, minds, and eyes towards Heaven (on things above – Colossians 3:2), suffering will become an inescapable part of our lives.

- He suffered because He stood for the truth. He was chastised for speaking the truth to the Jewish leaders on the night of His arrest (St. Matthew 26:64). Standing on the side of Jesus will not win us any popularity contests with the world.

- Jesus shared in the pain of our suffering for the sins we have committed and that have been committed against us. He shares in the pain of every child who ever lost a parent because of drug abuse and with every woman who is grieving because she bought the lie that abortion was the better choice. He is grieving with me in my pain of being sexually abused as a child. He also shares in the pain of my uncle who molested me. This may be hard for some to understand, but once the Lord brought me past my anger, I often wonder at the painful shame that my uncle must have gone through. Firstly, I wonder what happened to my uncle that brought him to the point where he became sick enough to molest a child; secondly, I wonder at the shame he must have gone through after being confronted by my family; and lastly, I wonder at the grief he must have gone through for committing such a shameful act. My uncle died from complications with AIDS when I was a teenager. I cannot help but think that his life was one of much suffering.

- Jesus suffers when He witnesses us commit sins against one another. He is grieved when He sees us turning our backs on Him and embracing the lies of the devil, the world, and of our flesh. He grieves when we do not deny our own fleshly desires and pick up our crosses and follow Him daily (St. Matthew 6:24). Jesus grieves at the sin that my uncle committed against me, and, likewise, He is grieved at the sin that was committed against my uncle that led him on the path that he chose. I do not believe that people are born as child molesters. I believe that my uncle, along with every other pedophile, committed such grievous sins as a result of a sickness inflicted by the experiences of their own lives. Sin is part of our human nature, but it is also very much perpetuated from person to person and from generation to generation. Again, this may sound strange to some, but I have not only suffered because of the sin that my uncle committed against me; I also suffer along with my uncle. I grieve deeply for this man who chose our Mother Mary as his patron saint at his confirmation into the Church. What went so painfully wrong?

We are all united as one in Christ, we are part of His Body, and as we learn to walk in love, we begin to feel the other parts of the body. When we become born again, God's Spirit knits us into one body of believers, connecting us into one nervous system.

12. As a body is one though it has many parts, and all the parts of the body, though many, are one body, so also Christ.

13. For in one Spirit we were all baptized in-to one body, whether Jews or Greeks, slaves or free persons, and we were all given to drink of one Spirit.

14. Now the body is not a single part, but many.

15. If a foot should say, "Because I am not a hand I do not belong to the body," it does not for this reason belong any less to the body.

16. Or if an ear should say, "Because I am not an eye I do not belong to the body," it does not for this reason belong any less to the body.

17. If the whole body were an eye, where would the hearing be? If the whole body were hearing, where would the sense of smell be?

18. But as it is, God placed the parts, each one of them, in the body as he intended.

19. If they were all one part, where would the body be?

20. But as it is, there are many parts, yet one body.

21. The eye cannot say to the hand, "I do not need you," nor again the head to the feet, "I do not need you."

22. Indeed, the parts of the body that seem to be weaker are all the more necessary,

23. and those parts of the body that we consider less honorable we surround with greater honor, and our less presentable parts are treated with greater propriety,

25. so that there may be no division in the body, but that the parts may have same concern for one another.

26. If [one] part suffers, all the parts suffer with it; if one part is honored, all the parts share its joy.

1 Corinthians 12:12-26

Fruit of The Spirit

~

As we allow the Holy Spirit to nurture our relationships as part of the Body of Christ, we develop evidences that God is at work in our lives. These evidences are described as *"Fruit of the Spirit"* by St. Paul in his letter to the Galatians.

22. In contrast, the fruit of the Spirit is love, joy, peace, patience, kindness, generosity, faithfulness,

23. gentleness, self-control. Against such there is no law.

24. Now those who belong to Christ [Jesus] have crucified their flesh with its passions and desires.

25. If we live in the Spirit, let us also follow the Spirit.

Galatians 5: 22-25

Life in Christ is not all suffering. On the contrary, it should be a life filled with the Fruits of the Spirit; it should be life filled with joy, peace, and love. Mother Teresa of Calcutta, who has been an inspiration to many who are seeking the path of Love (God), said, *"every time you smile at someone, it is an action of love, a gift to that person, a beautiful thing."* When we walk in the Spirit and draw closer to God, we cannot help but grow in love with Him and with His children. I know, speaking for myself, I have been very difficult to love at times, but Jesus through His saints (everyday people whom I have encountered in His Church, Protestant and Catholic alike) has drawn me to Himself with a love that I never expected and most certainly never deserved. To love the sinner is to hate the sin that threatens to kill. In this fallen world, love coexists with hate, and joy with sadness, they go hand in hand. Sadly enough, before the fall, Adam and Eve lived in perfect love and joy without either hate or sadness. These two emotions come with the *"knowledge of good and evil."*

17. except the tree of knowledge of good and evil. From that tree you shall not eat; when you eat from it you shall die.

Genesis 2:17

The deeper we fall in love with Jesus, the deeper we are immersed in His Spirit and the more we become vulnerable in our emotions. We become fully alive, and share completely in Christ - completely in His joy and completely in His suffering. We cannot have it one way or the other. Jesus came to give us the fullness of life in the Spirit.

10. A thief comes only to steal and slaughter and destroy; I came so that they might have life and have it more abundantly.

Jesus Christ – St. John 10:10

To those who walk in this life according to the flesh and keep their hearts and minds focused on what joys they will receive from the world, the thought of the sufferings of Purgatory is terrifying. They are not only terrifying to unbelievers, but also to believers who have gauged their spiritual growth by their prosperity in the things of this world. To those who are focused on things above - those who turn their backs on the prosperity of this world and count suffering with Christ all joy - the sufferings of Purgatory are a welcome way of drawing closer to the sweet presence of our Lord.

2. Consider it all joy, my brothers, when you encounter various trials,

3. For you know that the testing of your faith produces perseverance.

4. And let perseverance be perfect, so that you may be perfect and complete, lacking in nothing.

5. But if any of you lacks wisdom, he should

ask God who gives to all generously and un-grudgingly, and he will be given it.

6. But he should ask in faith, not doubting, for the one who doubts is like a wave of the sea that is driven and tossed about by the wind.

7. For that person must not suppose that he will receive anything from the Lord,

8. since he is a man of two minds, unstable in all his ways.

9. The brother in lowly circumstances, should take pride in his high standing,

10. and the rich one in his lowliness, for he will pass away "like the flower of the field."

11. For the sun comes up with its scorching heat and dries up the grass, its flower droops, and the beauty of its appearance vanishes. So will the rich person fade away in the midst of his pursuits.

James 12:2-11

The above portion of Scripture is often misinterpreted by certain Christian movements and used to infuse a worldly agenda into the Christian culture. They twist St. James' words to mean the exact opposite of his intended meaning. He is encouraging the readers to ask for joy in their trials if they have not received the joy of the Lord in their circumstances already. He is not admonishing believers to pray for wealth as a means of relief from whatever type of trial they may be experiencing. He is admonishing the believer to ask for the wisdom to see the joy in the trial. St. James, actually, in verses 10 and 11, gives reasons why having faith in the wealth of this world has its pitfalls and conversely elevates the *"brother in lowly circumstances"* and tells him to *"take pride in his high standing."* This will be impossible for the carnally minded person to understand and accept and goes completely against the grain of the world system.

I would like to share that on most mornings I go into my office and read the daily readings of the Church on the United States Conference of Catholic Bishops' website. The following is today's (September 18, 2015) first reading just as it appears on the site. I added the scripture above from the Book of St. James and comments yesterday morning. The longer I walk with our amazing Father in Heaven, the more it reinforces my belief that nothing in this life happens by chance. Somehow, way beyond my understanding, within our being given complete free will, He still has *"it"* all worked out.

Reading 1

Beloved:

Teach and urge these things.

Whoever teaches something different

and does not agree with the sound words of our Lord Jesus Christ

and the religious teaching

is conceited, understanding nothing,

and has a morbid disposition for arguments and verbal disputes.

From these come envy, rivalry, insults, evil suspicions,

and mutual friction among people with corrupted minds,

who are deprived of the truth,

supposing religion to be a means of gain.

Indeed, religion with contentment is a great gain.

For we brought nothing into the world,

just as we shall not be able to take anything out of it.

If we have food and clothing, we shall be content with that.

Those who want to be rich are falling into temptation and into a trap

and into many foolish and harmful desires,

which plunge them into ruin and destruc-

tion.

For the love of money is the root of all evils,

and some people in their desire for it have strayed from the faith

and have pierced themselves with many pains.

But you, man of God, avoid all this.

Instead, pursue righteousness, devotion,

faith, love, patience, and gentleness.

Compete well for the faith.

Lay hold of eternal life,

to which you were called when you made the noble confession

in the presence of many witnesses.

1 Timothy 6:2C-12

These are the little kisses from God, often seemingly insignificant, that let us know that we are on the right track.

So far, included in St. Paul's list of the fruits of the Spirit, we have discussed love and joy. The third virtue on St. Paul's list is peace (Galatians 5:22). *"Peace,"* the catchphrase of the 1960s, was and is a word used out of context for many, if not most. Most people can relate to the image of a long-haired hippie with tie-dyed t-shirt holding up his index and middle fingers on one hand (the universal sign for peace) and his thumb sticking out on the other hand as he hitchhikes down the road. Peace to this guy most likely meant something completely different than it meant to St. Paul. Peace to the generation that attended Woodstock and partook in the *"Summer of Love"* meant *"let me do my thing, and I will let you do your thing"* or, in the vernacular, *"don't judge me, and I won't judge you."* Yes, the Church teaches us not to judge, but the inference is not *"sin as you please, and all will be well."*

The word *"peace"* that St. Paul describes as a fruit of the Spirit is intended to communicate a word that means to have a sense that all is well because we trust that our Father in Heaven has everything in our lives under control, not the sense that we are not being judged and can do exactly what we want when we feel like. This is not to say that the world cannot understand peace. Many experience moments of a sense of well-being; for example, most can relate to the feeling that comes over a person while watching a sunset out over the water or while taking a quiet walk in the woods in the morning. These times can feel almost spiritual to even the most committed atheist, but they are fleeting.

The moment the *"stuff"* of this life raises its

ugly head, that feeling of peace is the first to flee. Love can be completely unconditional, but peace is always conditional. We have peace in our financial future because we have large savings accounts, or we have peace in our marriages because we have developed trust that our spouses will be faithful. Likewise, we develop the peace in our lives that St. Paul has listed in this text by trusting that God has all things in our lives under control. As of all of the fruits of the Spirit, they ripen and mature as we walk closer to God. They are the evidence of His Spirit reigning in our lives. The verse that comes to mind is from Psalm 23: *"Even though I walk through the valley of the shadow of death, I will fear no evil, for you are with me; your rod and your staff comfort me" (Psalm 23: 24).* To understand this verse, you must understand what the rod and staff meant in the mind of David, the writer of this psalm.

The rod is a symbol of discipline or correction. Most people do not like being disciplined or corrected, but most mature adults can speak to, through the hand of experience, the fact that both are necessary for a child to grow into a well balanced, mature person. The old adage *"to spare the rod is to spoil the child"* (Proverbs 13:24) should be popping into the minds of many reading this. As we grow in our faith, we should learn to view suffering in this way. God does not find some type of sick pleasure in seeing us suffer; He understands that sometimes suffering is the only way we will learn. Some of us may have heard our parents say *"this is going to hurt me more than it will hurt you"* just before we received a spanking. As a child, this makes no sense at all, but as we grow in maturity, we understand that most parents hate to see their children suffer the pain of a spanking but understand that it is necessary at times. Likewise, as we mature in our faith, we should learn to recognize that the suffering that we experience while we are being corrected by our loving Father in Heaven is for our good and should become a welcomed comfort.

4. In your struggle against sin you have not yet resisted to the point of shedding blood.

5. You have also forgotten the exhortation addressed to you as sons: "My son, do not disdain the discipline of the Lord or lose heart when reproved by him;

6. for whom the Lord loves, he disciplines; he scourges every son he acknowledges.

7. Endure your trials as "discipline"; God treats you as sons. For what "son" is there whom his father does not discipline?

Hebrews 12:4-7

The staff was something that was also very familiar to David. This was a tool that he would have used while tending his father's sheep as a youth. A shepherd's staff was used to guide stubborn and quite often not very bright sheep. This is most likely why the Lord refers to His children throughout scripture as sheep. The staff could either be used to prod with its straight end or to pull a sheep along with the opposite end, which was bent over in the shape of a large hook. The imagery that David is communicating in this psalm carries through to this day in the form of a bishop's hook. Our modern day bishops in the Church carry a bishop's staff, with the end that is held upward called the bishop's hook, during most ceremonial functions. The hook, of course, is a symbol of the bishop being the shepherd of his flock. The term has even carried over into architecture. Many architectural features that are in the shape of a hook will be called bishop's hooks. I have definitely felt the hook of the Lord's staff around my neck, and I must be honest, I am still working on finding comfort in the experience at times. The other purpose for the staff is to protect the flock from predators. A sheep that has been under the guidance of the shepherd for any length of time will have witnessed the protection that the staff provides in the hands of the shepherd. When the flock sees a predator, it instinctively calls out with bleats and runs toward the shepherd knowing that he is where their protection lies. The image that the psalmist is attempting to communicate is that of a sheep laying down in a green pasture completely at peace, without a worry in its mind, because the shepherd is standing in watch. Without the presence of the shepherd and staff, there would be no peace for the sheep. Peace is completely conditional.

The peace that develops through faith in God is completely foreign to the carnal mind. During persecution, confrontation, or periods of anguish, people of the world who are carnally minded will typically fall into despair either by responding in anger or shrinking back in fear, quite often with the aid of a pharmaceutical crutch. Thus, when unbelievers see Christians at peace during such times, they take notice. We display the peace of God's love in our lives through our actions. The world takes notice of someone who is not coming apart at the seams when he loses his job or has just suffered the loss of a loved one, someone who trusts completely in his or her God.

This type of peace can be more substantial than all of the gold in the world. This is the type of behavior of which the world is completely without understanding. Faith is the evidence of things unseen, but peace is the evidence of faith. Peace is the substance that gives believers the courage to choose to be shot and killed rather than denounce Christ. Peace is what causes martyrs to sing out with hymns of joy as they are being burned at the stake or having their flesh ripped off piece by piece. Believers are given a supernatural indwelling of the Holy Spirit in their time of need, not just to endure suffering, but also to display a peace that passes all understanding.

4. Rejoice in the Lord always. I shall say it again: rejoice!

5. Your kindness should be known to all. The Lord is near.

6. Have no anxiety at all, but in everything, by prayer and petition, with thanksgiving, make your requests known to God.

7. Then the peace of God that surpasses all understanding will guard your hearts and minds in Christ Jesus.

This is the peace that Jesus displayed on the Cross of which the entire world took notice and still does to this day.

1. Therefore, since we are surrounded by so great a cloud of witnesses, let us rid ourselves of every burden and sin that clings to us and persevere in running the race that lies before us

2. while keeping our eyes fixed on Jesus, the leader and perfecter of faith. For the sake of the joy that lay before him he endured the cross, despising its shame, and has taken his seat at the right of the throne of God.

Hebrews 12:1-2

As described in the passage above, Jesus did not find peace or joy in his circumstances nor did He embrace the shame of sin; He despised the shame of sin. The joy that He found was, in fact, that His home in Heaven awaited Him and that He would have destroyed the grip of death by the time the day was over. It was a joy that was displayed as peace. He rested in the fact that His Father in Heaven had everything under control.

He took the Cross without uttering a word in His own defense. He was mocked by the crowd, and He was even mocked by one of the two men who were being crucified along with him.

37. And they placed over his head the written charge against him: This is Jesus, the King of the Jews.

38. Two revolutionaries were crucified with him, one on his right and the other on his left.

39. Those passing by reviled him, shaking their heads

40. and saying, "You who would destroy the temple and rebuild it in three days, save yourself, if you are the Son of God, [and] come down from the cross!"

41. Likewise the chief priests with the scribes and elders mocked him and said,

42. "He saved others; he cannot save himself. So he is the king of Israel! Let him come down from the cross now, and we will believe in him.

43. He trusted in God; let him deliver him now if he wants him. For he said, 'I am the Son of God.'"

44. The revolutionaries who were crucified with him also kept abusing him in the same way.

It is obvious that most witnessing this scene knew who Jesus was - they had followed his story on CNN and Twitter - so they were obviously very frustrated at His silence. It is always easier for a bully to strike an innocent person if he can taunt that person into aggression. Most have witnessed the scene from the schoolyard: a bully casts insults about the mother of a kid who is half his size so that he can feel justified in hitting the weaker kid - the weaker kid reached his boiling point and strikes out in anger. The bully typically is doing nothing more than trying to show how strong he is through intimidation because he, in all reality, has no confidence in himself or his surroundings. A strongman who is confident in his power does not feel the need to prove himself. The thing that the folks in this crowd were learning was that Jesus does not have a boiling point; He is the *"baddest cat"* in the schoolyard, and He knows it.

They also did not understand that they were not just railing against the man on the cross, they were furthermore casting insults at God Himself, and that Jesus' strength is in weakness. When we are weak, we allow God to be strong. What if Jesus had jumped down off of the Cross and kicked some tail, shooting lightning from His Eyes, which I am absolutely sure He was capable? Would that have displayed that Jesus had faith in His Father? The answer is obvious: not at all! We display the awesome power of God's love in the same way: through our weakness. We actually prove our strength through our weakness, which is displayed through the peace that passes all understanding (Philippians 4:7) and with the same joy that strengthened our Savior on the Cross.

9. but he said to me, "My grace is sufficient for you, for power is made perfect in weakness." I will rather boast most gladly of my weaknesses, in order that the power of Christ may dwell with me.

10. Therefore, I am content with weaknesses, insults, hardships, persecutions, and constraints, for the sake of Christ; for when I am weak, then I am strong.

2 Corinthians 12:9-10

There may be some reading this who are wondering what suffering from persecution has to do with Purgatory? The answer is everything. It is because of sin in the world that all suffering takes place whether it is from persecution, from being sinned against, or from the sins that we have committed ourselves. We can walk through this life with our consciences being seared and ignoring the pain and suffering of this world, or we can share in its suffering by embracing the joy that stands before us and knocks at the door of our hearts in the Person of Jesus Christ.

18. I consider that the sufferings of this present time are as nothing compared with the glory to be revealed for us.

19. For creation awaits with eager expectation the revelation of the children of God;

20. for creation was made subject to futility, not of its own accord but because of the one who subjected it, in hope

21. that creation itself would be set free from slavery to corruption and share in the glorious freedom of the children of God.

22. We know that all creation is groaning in labor pains even until now;

23. and not only that, but we ourselves, who have the firstfruits of the Spirit, we also groan within ourselves as we wait for adoption, the redemption of our bodies.

24. For in hope we were saved. Now hope that sees for itself is not hope. For who hopes for what one sees?

25. But if we hope for what we do not see, we wait with endurance.

In verse 21 above, St. Paul speaks of being set free from *"slavery to corruption and share in the glorious freedom of the children of God."* What are we set free from, and how are we set free? We are set free from the bondage of sin, and we are set free from the hold on our character and the penalty of sins that we have committed. Please understand that we do not only need healing from individual sins committed against us and from the sins that we have committed, but also from the very nature of sin. What good is it to be forgiven of the sin of fornication if lust still burns within our hearts? Christ died for that sin of adultery, and we are forgiven, but if we still struggle with lust, we are still in bondage. How can this be? Christ died to set us free. Did Jesus pour out His Blood for nothing? Jesus will free us from the nature of sin, but as it is with most people, is an ongoing process of healing, in His perfect time.

20. Now if [I] do what I do not want, it is no longer I who do it, but sin that dwells in me.

21. So, then, I discover the principle that when I want to do right, evil is at hand.

173

22. For I take delight in the law of God, in my inner self,

23. but I see in my members another principle at war with the law of my mind, taking me captive to the law of sin that dwells in my members.

Romans 7:20-23

Remember, forgiveness is the beginning of healing. What is it to take up our cross and follow Him daily? Is it to expect to have one bad day after another full of persecution and suffering? Not exactly! All sins ever committed, and that ever will be committed are against God. God came to Earth in the form of the man Jesus and poured out His Blood as an offering for the forgiveness of all of the sins of the world in the hope that we would accept His offering and be healed. This was not conditional. He did not say if you will ask for forgiveness I will die on a cross for you; no, He died first in Hope through love. If we truly become partakers in the suffering of Christ, we must suffer with Him in His sacrifice. We must forgive those who sin against us before they even ask in hope that they would be healed. Yes, we must lay down our right to be right and lay any desire for retribution at the foot of the cross.

"To the person who strikes you on one cheek,

offer the other one as well, and from the person who takes your cloak, do not withhold even your tunic" (St. Luke 6:29). This type of forgiveness is only possible through the Holy Spirit's being active in our lives. This type of forgiveness goes completely against the fallen nature of man. This is one of the ways that we take up our cross.

I have every right to be angry with my uncle for abusing me, and it would be understood in the world's eyes if I sought justice through vindication. Those of us who pray for justice, be careful. Justice would dictate that we would burn in hell for our sins. If our prayer is for grace, and grace is what we have all been offered through the Cross, then how can we accept the grace given to us through Christ's suffering and insist on justice for our brothers and sisters (St. Matthew 21-35)?

Isaiah, given a vision of our forgiveness and healing through the Holy Spirit, said:

5. But he was pierced for our sins, crushed for our iniquity. He bore the punishment that makes us whole, By his wounds we were healed.

Isaiah 53:5

Jesus led the way. He laid down His life and poured out His Blood for our forgiveness; now we must follow Him in forgiveness. Healing began at the Cross, but it is up to us to carry on the work of His Kingdom. Isaiah is not talking about our physical bodies in the above passage; he is talking about the healing of our spirits and our souls. God does heal people physically, but that is not to what the prophet is referring. Every time we pray the Lord's prayer, we pray:

10. your kingdom come, your will be done, on earth as in heaven

11. Give us today our daily bread;

12. and forgive us our debts, as we forgive our debtors;

St. Matthew 6:10-12

I have forgiven my uncle. And I have not only forgiven him, but I also pray for his complete healing and that we will be reconciled one day in God's kingdom. Somehow I have a sense that we have already been reconciled in our spirits through the ministry of the Holy Spirit, but one day my hope is to put my arms around his neck and tell him I love him in person. This longing and this love in my heart could have only come about through the ministry of the Holy Spirit that was poured out on us through the redeeming sacrifice that Jesus made for us on the Cross. The pain and suffering that I have gone through during my time of healing through the Holy Spirit was more than I ever thought possible, but the joy and peace I have experienced could have only come about as a result of sharing in the suffering of Christ Jesus (1 Peter 1:6-8).

Whether it be here, during this age, or in Heaven, it is my prayer that you experience that same joy.

Physical Suffering

~

There is another element of suffering that we experience during our captivity in this foreign land that I would be remiss in not mentioning. It is the suffering of the sick and injured. Many in this life are born into great suffering through illness or abnormalities that occur in the womb. Others experience sickness or injury along the journey. Many are innocent victims of this fallen world, and others suffer from their own misguided actions. As the Church, it is our duty to share in the suffering of the sick and injured by ministering to their needs. We are all in this together. We cannot separate whom from what from where. We must just simply strive to minister to the suffering of this fallen world through our love for Christ and compassion for the hurting. God did not create sickness. Sickness came about as a result of the fall and is perpetuated through sin. I am not saying that people are born into sickness as punishment for sin—not at all. As a matter of fact, I do not understand why a child is born with cancer or physical disabilities, why a person develops Lou Gehrig's disease, or why innocent people die in a hurricane. What I do know, though, is that it is often grievous beyond our understanding. What I am absolutely confident of is that Jesus thinks that they are grievous too and that He will heal every sickness and injury in His perfect time. Our Lord wept along with Martha and Mary at the news of Lazarus' death (St. John 11:35). This is where faith comes in; we must trust that the suffering of this world is not worthy to compare to the glory that will be *"revealed in us"* in His Kingdom (Romans 8:18). Part of the good news is that God will give us new incorruptible bodies in Heaven, not made of this corruptible flesh, but of spirit as the heavenly hosts (I Corinthians 15:42-53). We must trust that this God of ours, Who created us and loves us enough to suffer with us, has a perfect reason and purpose for everything. He doesn't ever wish sickness on a child, but through His love, He can make something good from our suffering.

Joy in Suffering

~

Early on during my time of healing, which is still in process, through the Holy Spirit, I was ministered to by a nearly 500-year-old woman in a very unexpected way. At that time, the thought of being ministered to by someone who was dead was completely foreign. I guess I had not come to the belief that the dead in Christ are not, actually, dead, but alive in Heaven. As a Protestant, we talked about people going to Heaven when they died but based on our actions I am not sure that we wholeheartedly believed that it is true. I am not so sure that this is not the reason that most Protestants have an issue with praying to the Saints.

If we are to follow Christ on Earth and have given our lives for the Gospel in ministering to God's people, would that change when we pass from this life to the next? Did the ministry focus of Jesus Change? My understanding of the way that the Saints, who have gone on to be with the Lord, minister to us changed the day I met St. Teresa of Avila. Whether by her written word or, as I prefer to believe, her active intercession in Heaven, this woman has changed my life. She reached through the veil and touched me at a time when I needed to be ministered to in a very real way. There were days, weeks, and even months when I could feel her presence.

St. Teresa was, and I hope still is, a very intense individual. Her writing is very charged with emotion and riddled with raw expression that can be hard to follow. I can imagine that being with her in person may have been exhausting at times. I can picture God looking over at the angels and saying something along the lines of, *"Look, here is one I can use to do great things,"* or *"wait until you see what I do with this one."*

She wrote the way she lived: with passion. I have no doubt that she carried that energy into Heaven and still ministers in the same way. St. Teresa, pray for us.

It is through her unfettered expression and burning desire to press into the Heart of God that she has left behind a wealth of writings for us to read and to grow through. She has been given the distinct honor of being considered a Doctor of the Church. I understand that her title was given her due to her academic accomplishments in the ministry of contemplative prayer, but I have, definitely, received healing through her legacy and intercession.

It was during one of my darkest points in 2008 that I read *"Transverberation"* for the fist time. The *"Transverberation"* is the title given to St. Teresa's account of receiving a vision from our Lord of an angel sent to pierce her with a spear, cleansing her with the fire of Gods' Love.

One of the things I love about the Catholic Church is that She always has these *"really cool"* names for everything. It couldn't have just been titled *"St. Teresa's very cool vision"* or *"Teresa and the Fiery Angel."* I can imagine a bunch of priests sitting in a room at the Vatican discussing what to call the vision. *"Okay, brothers, we need to come up with something way cooler than the last one."*

Okay, off of the rabbit trail.

I did not understand all of the implications of the vision the first time I read it, but I was undone just the same. It was as if the Holy Sprit used the vision to crack open my chest and push into my heart the truth of God's healing touch.

The following is a portion of the *"Transver-beration:"*

"I saw in his hand a long spear of gold, and at the iron's point there seemed to be a little fire. He appeared to me to be thrust-

ing it at times into my heart and to pierce my very entrails; when he drew it out, he seemed to draw them out also, and to leave me all on fire with a great love of God. The pain was so great, that it made me moan; and yet so surpassing was the sweetness of this excessive pain, that I could not wish to be rid of it. The soul is satisfied now with nothing less than God. The pain is not bodily, but spiritual; though the body has its share in it, even a large one. It is a caressing of love so sweet which now takes place between the soul and God, that I pray God of His goodness to make him experience it who may think that I am lying."

St. Teresa of Avila, The Book of Her Life, Chapter 19

As I have mentioned above, I read this for the first time soon after I started going through my *"big breakdown,"* during one of the darkest periods of my life. Before I read this, I was not sure that I wasn't going through some, type of, delusional break. I had spent the past twenty or so years before learning what I thought was true about God. When I would start to share what I was going through with other believers, I was most often, cut short very quickly and, told that

God does not operate in the way I was describing. I thought I knew what God's touch felt like. Either I was feeling God's Hand in my situation and hearing His voice, or I had never known His touch or heard Him speak a word.

I could hear Him so clearly and feel Him so presently at times that it was uncomfortable because my circumstances were not in keeping with the way I perceived that God operated in the lives of His children. Stepping forward several years, I now read the scripture with a completely different understanding of who God is and of the way He interacts with His children. It is as if I was missing huge sections of the story. I often describe it as if God was filling in the missing words that I never knew could have existed. Now I see that the way He was dealing with me was not so different than the way He has dealt with people throughout history. I just needed to have the scales removed from my eyes to see the truth. Mine did not just fall away, though; it was a slow painful process (Acts 9:18).

As I started to process in my mind St. Teresa's vision, I began to understand that the pain of suffering is the way of the Cross and that it was perfectly normal to feel God's touch during the confusion of healing. Our Lord's touch is the only way through those darkest hours, as a lighthouse gives aid to a ship during a storm. He does not take away the storm, but He is a beacon of hope through the comfort of His touch leading us at times into the roughest waters before we are able to experience the calm of His healing. She showed me that it is perfectly normal to experience His joy and peace while we are suffering. This does not make us crazy; it makes us loved. Please understand that the feeling of God's presence does not remove any of the pain. Actually, in many ways, His presence increases the pain. When we walk through this world indwelled with perfect love, the implications of man's fallen state into sin becomes more grievous and painful.

We Suffer Together

~

Love and suffering are directly proportionate to one another. When someone we love is suffering, we cannot help but grieve right along with him or her. When my wife and I were separated, I was very angry with her, but I could not help but be moved by the pain that the situation was putting her through. Her pain was a huge influence in the healing of our relationship and the saving of our marriage. She would speak to me in my dreams, in which I could see her in pain. The Lord loves us perfectly and comes to our aid in the same way. He will not leave us in pain. During the time of our separation, I came to a new understanding of my wife and myself being one flesh and of the way we are all connected spiritually. This is not some type of *"new age"* spirituality. The Word of God very clearly says that we are one body (St. Mark 10:8) and that when one suffers, we all suffer (1 Corinthians 12:26).

When I was going through my *"big break-down,"* it affected my entire family and many friends who were close enough to have the unfortunate experience of being around me while I was *"dying to myself."* The sin that had been committed against me approximately 41 years earlier did not just hurt me; it hurt my wife, my children, and all of the people whom I hurt along the way. Sin is not a single act; it is a sickness that infects every one of us and is handed down from generation to generation, from person to person. This does not mean that sin would not reign in the life of a person who was raised completely separated from other people. We are born into sin, completely self-centered in our nature, separated from God. It is only through divine union with our Creator that this sickness can be cured. Our self-centered nature is what causes us to perpetuate sinful behavior.

In Exodus, Moses talks about the love of God continuing for a thousand generations but explains that the iniquity for the wicked deeds of His people will be handed down to the *"third and the fourth generation"* (Exodus 34:7, RSVCE). Some versions of the Catholic Bible use the word *"punish" in place of "iniquity."* Whichever version you chose to follow, the intent of the verse is to communicate that God loves us very much and will never stop loving us, but the sins of our fathers affect us in a very real way. God does not punish us for another person's sins; however, other people's sins hurt others in a real way. Put simply, fathers, think before you go and do something stupid because the consequences could very well fall upon your children.

As I stated above, I often wonder what happened to my uncle to cause him to be sick enough to molest a toddler. For how many generations has this sickness been handed down? Did he have a sick family member who molested him? I have no idea, and there is nothing I can do to change the past, but I can work on changing the future by clinging to my only hope, Who is Christ Jesus, of breaking this cycle of sin. Jesus is our hope. It is by His stripes that we are healed (Isaiah 53:5). It is by sharing in His suffering that we can be Jesus to others by laying down our own lives, our own selfish desires, and picking up our crosses and following Him daily.

Our Hope in Jesus

~

Consider those who pass from this life to the next who have never begun the process of being purged from the pain of sin. Consider those who die, who have never faced the pain of this life in any other way than through self-medicating. As we draw closer to God, the fire of the Holy Spirit cleanses us of the filth of this world. There are those who are just going through the motions day to day. Many of us may be going to church, and we may love Jesus, but the pain of this life has become too much, and we have spent a lifetime running from our emotions.

Consider those who are thrown into eternity (because of an unexpected death) with their naked and bleeding spirits, covered in the filth of this world, whose only comfort in this life was the fulfillment of sensual desire? The pain and suffering of those of us who find ourselves in this state will be unthinkable.

Think about the drug addict who is cut off from the source of his comfort *"cold turkey."* The pain is often unbearable and can cause physical death. In that place, we will be stripped of our bodies and will no longer be able to find comfort in physical relationships, alcohol, drugs, or shopping sprees. We will be exposed, just as we are, with nowhere to hide from the God Who loves us enough to heal us from all of the *"stuff"* of this life no matter how much it hurts.

Consider a man or a woman who has lost a spouse after being married for 50 or 60 years, which is the majority of a lifetime. Quite often, the remaining spouse will die within a relatively short period of time. I have heard it said that that spouse died from a broken heart or that he or she just loses the desire to live. When we focus the majority of our thoughts and desires on something or someone for the better part of a lifetime, it is perfectly understandable that the loss of that thing or that person will be extremely painful. Thus, spending the majority of our time focusing on this life will be a very poor invest-ment considering that we will be spending eter-nity with God in Heaven, or on the New Earth.

I am not saying that dying of a broken heart is a bad thing after losing a wife with whom you have spent the majority of your life. I would say that such a person loved and loved well. What I am saying, though, is that we need to spend the majority of our time focusing on things above and painfully longing for Heaven (Colossians

3:2) instead of focusing on things below (this life) and painfully missing this life, which we will never see again after we move on to the next.

> *19. Do not store up for yourselves treasures on earth, where moth and decay destroy, and thieves break in and steal.*

> *20. But store up treasures in heaven, where neither moth nor decay destroys, nor thieves break in and steal.*

> *21. For where your treasure is, there also will your heart be.*

> *St. Matthew 6: 19-21*

Many may be thinking at this point, *"What about Jesus? Won't He be there when I enter into the Heaven? Won't He be there to comfort me?"* The answer is yes. He will be there and is already there with your spirit. Many years ago I was sitting on a plane on the tarmac at Pensacola Airport waiting to take off. The flight was delayed due to bad weather, and I was gripped with fear. I am afraid of flying in good weather, but the thought of taking off and flying into a storm put me on edge. I will never forget the emotions involved. I was praying for Jesus to comfort me. He very clearly answered me that He would, and He did, but He followed His answer with words that changed the direction of my life. He said, *"Bill, today I will comfort you, but the day will come when I will need to be your comfort."*

Praying for the Dead

~

1. The souls of the righteous are in the hand of God, and no torment shall touch them.

2. They seemed, in the view of the foolish, to be dead; and their passing away was thought an affliction

3. and their going forth from us, utter destruction. But they are in peace.

4. For if to others, indeed, they seem punished, yet is their hope full of immortality;

5. Chastised a little, they shall be greatly blessed, because God tried them and found them worthy of Himself.

6. As gold in the furnace, He proved them, and as sacrificial offerings He took them to himself.

7. In the time of their judgment they shall shine and dart about as sparks through stubble;

8. They shall judge nations and rule over peoples, and the LORD shall be their King forever.

9. Those who trust in Him shall understand truth, and the faithful shall abide with Him in love: Because grace and mercy are with His holy ones, and His care is with the elect.

10. But the wicked shall receive a punishment to match their thoughts, since they neglected righteousness and forsook the LORD.

11. For those who despise wisdom and instruction are doomed. Vain is their hope, fruitless their labors, and worthless their works.

12. Their wives are foolish and their children wicked, accursed their brood.

Wisdom 3:1-12

Something that I feel that most people fail to remember, who take issue with praying for the Dead in Christ, is that they are not dead! The term *"Dead in Christ"* is an oxymoron. What people are actually trying to communicate when they say the *"Dead in Christ,"* should more appropriately be termed as "those who have died to this life and have entered into the fullness of life in Christ."

Unfortunately, as a Protestant, for over 20 years of studying the Bible, I never read the above verses from the Book of Wisdom. The Book of Wisdom was removed from the Bible by Martin Luther during the Reformation. Verses 5 and 6 undisputedly speak of a place where the Just are purified after they have died to this life. My Protestant brothers and sisters, please take the time to read the seven books of the Bible that were removed from the Protestant Bible. At the very least, they may shed some light as to why we as Catholics believe some of the things that we believe. These seven books are referred to as *"Deuterocanonical"* by Catholics and were composed during the last two hundred years before Christ. They are not considered prophetic in inspiration but were considered for over the thousand-year history of the early Church, before the Reformation, to be an integral part of the inerrant word of God. Oddly, a little-known fact is that the 1611 edition of the King James Bible in English contained these books, in a separate section labeled *"Apocrypha."* They were later omitted in 1885. I am very thankful for Martin Luther's stand on certain issues. I believe that he was God's instrument for change within the Church, but on this issue, I believe he overstepped his authority.

Praying for the dead who are not in Christ would be foolish (Wisdom 3:2), but considering it is not our place to even consider if someone is in hell, praying for the dead should not be an issue for anybody.

6. But the righteousness that comes from faith says, "Do not say in your heart, 'Who will go up into heaven?' (that is, to bring Christ down)

7. or 'Who will go down into the abyss?' (that is, to bring Christ up from the dead)."

Romans 10:6-7

Our place on this earth is to walk in grace and mercy, being ministers of hope to everyone with whom we come in contact. When my father-in-law was dying of cancer, my wife and I brought him home to spend the last few weeks of his life among his family. Family flew in from around the country. The man was a patron in a very real sense of the word. He loved and was loved by many. When he was in the hospital and later moved into our home, my wife, Mary, and I would take turns being by his side. He was never left alone, and while we were watching over him, we would be continuously covering him with prayer and hymns. One of our family members expressed a little frustration with the fact that we were praying for him to be healed when it was obvious that in the flesh, this man continued to get sick and was within a few days of passing away to the next life. Believe me, I understand the frustration. When we are upset, we typically do not want someone from the *"happy clappy club"* dancing around trying to spread joy. Our answer to this person is that we are ministers of life and of hope. That is what we do! That is Who Christ is. He brings hope to the world in which there is no hope. He ministers to the sick and brings life to the dying.

It is not our place as believers in any way to even think in our hearts whether another person is in hell or will be going to hell. Likewise, it is not our place to say if a person is in or is going to Heaven. To me, not to consider whether someone is in Heaven is the harder of the two. When someone dies, we typically like to think of that person as being in Heaven. Any of us who have walked in this life for any length of time have been to a funeral, and many of us have been to a funeral for someone who, how do I say it, wasn't always nice to the people around him or her. When sitting at one of these funerals, family and friends will slowly take the podium to say a few words about the deceased. The words spoken from the podium are almost always all of the good things that that person had done during his or her life on this earth. People will say the nicest thing about people at a funeral. Let's face the truth: they will turn the biggest scoundrel into a saint by the end of the service. How many of us have wanted to tiptoe up to the casket afterward and look in just to be sure that we were at the right funeral?

Hope is the anchor that keeps us tied steadfastly to sanity in this life. Without hope, we have nothing. For me, that hope is in the love of Christ. People who are desperate will cling to hope as a drowning person will cling to a life ring. As long as we have breath in our bodies, we should be ministers of hope.

Several years ago, we had a close family friend die in a tragic accident. It was one of those things in life that just grieves the soul beyond understanding! I am brought to tears just writing this. This young man became friends with my oldest son in high school, and through the years our families became friends. His name is Scott, and he is sorely missed by many. I will never forget walking into his memorial service to see his family just lost in pain. I was immersed in grief, and the first thing that came into my mind was a short prayer. *"Jesus, grab ahold of that boy and never let go."*

During that moment, Jesus was my only hope, my anchor. Sometimes in this life, unfortunately, it takes the greatest tragedies to show us our hearts. During that moment, I didn't want

Bible verses or reassuring words of comfort. I was desperately reaching for a life ring during the storm and grabbed ahold of Jesus. When we suffer a great loss, such as losing someone close to us, quite often, Heaven and Hell pass away within our hearts, and all that is left is Jesus standing with outstretched arms. Many Christians have theological principals that sound good on paper concerning life after death, but when the metal meets the fire, all of that crap burns into flame and is carried away in the wind along with all of the other dribble that has been taught throughout the ages. Our hope is in Christ alone, and as long as I am able, I will continue to pray for Scott.

I love the following quote from C.S. Lewis in his hallmark no-nonsense way of putting things.

"... Of course I pray for the dead. The action is so spontaneous, so all but inevitable, that only the most compulsive theological case against it would deter me. And I hardly know how the rest of my prayers would survive if those for the dead were forbidden. At our age, the majority of those we love best are dead. What sort of intercourse with God could I have if what I love best were unmentionable to him?"

Let's take Jesus out of the box in which most, including myself, have kept Him in at times. Many of the Old Testament Jews who lived by The Law, walked in the hope of Christ. They knew that the law in which they walked could bring nothing but death, yet they continued to walk the walk of the faithful and practiced the teachings of the law in every way possible in obedience to the God they loved. Let's take a look at David's writing in Psalm 130.

1. A song of ascents. Out of the depths I call to you, LORD;

2. Lord, hear my cry! May your ears be attentive to my cry for mercy.

3. If you, LORD, keep account of sins, Lord, who can stand?

4. But with you is forgiveness and so you are revered.

5. I wait for the LORD, my soul waits and I hope for his word.

6. My soul looks for the Lord more than sentinels for daybreak. More than sentinels for daybreak,

7. let Israel hope in the LORD, For with the

LORD is mercy, with him is plenteous re-demption,

8. And he will redeem Israel from all its sins.

Psalm 130:1-8

Soak in what you just read. David lived under, and was bound to, The Law and had absolutely no hope in that Law. He knew that he would most likely go to his grave long before the Christ would take the cross, consecrating the New Covenant and freeing him from death. Some would argue that David did not know about the crucifixion of Jesus Christ. David was given the inside track through the Holy Spirit to understand the promise of Christ over 1,000 years before He came (Psalm 22). He and the Holy Spirit were pretty tight back then, as I am sure they still are.

We should also understand that we should have no hope in the sacramental life of the Church. We should, definitely, adhere to the tenants of our faith. When we follow, in obedience, the sacramental life that the Church teaches, what we are saying by our actions is that we trust Jesus with our lives. We are saying, *"Jesus, I love you and will follow you wherever you go and do whatever you say."* The sacramental life is a way of living what is the absolute best for our lives, but we can adhere to every sacrament and still enter into hell. Our hope is in Jesus, not in the Church, and neither should it have been in the Law for those who lived before Christ established the Church (James 2:18). The Church has been established to lead the lost to faith in Christ.

Look at verse 6 above, *"more than sentinels wait for morning."* He wrote this twice. Remember this is a song. This was a point that he wanted to emphasize. A sentinel had the job of keeping watch for the enemy, typically from the parapet wall of a city or during times of battle from the best vantage point possible. If you happened to be blessed enough to draw the short straw and be selected for night watch, your job became exponentially more difficult and dangerous. The job was dangerous for two reasons. The first is that any force of men who were looking to attack at night would make taking out the sentinel their first priority, and during the time of David, they did not have spotlights, allowing an enemy to sneak up to the camp within an arrow's reach. The second reason was because if the Sentinel failed to warn the camp of the approach of an enemy force, he would be reprimanded severely, often by death. Daybreak was first and foremost in the mind of a sentinel who was pulling night duty. It was his ardent hope that the light would come before an enemy would approach.

For what was David watching? David was watching for Death, and he was standing in hope upon the parapet wall of life. When David died, did he go to hell because he had not received the Eucharist? I am being ridiculous. Remember that God works through the sacraments of the Church, but He is not bound by the sacraments. Our job is to be faithful and follow, and it is God's job to be God. Let me also reference, as we discussed previously (Romans 10:6-7), we are not even to consider whether someone is in Heaven or hell. That's a tough one, but keep working on it.

I know what some are thinking. The Church has canonized saints! Yes, She has and does. The first thing that I want to clarify is that when the Church canonizes a saint, She is not saying that that person is any better or more Holy than another. All who put our hope in Christ and follow Him as Lord are saints. Yes, that includes you, and it includes me. What She is doing is recognizing that person as living a life exemplary of the teachings of Christ and also recognizing any miracles attributed to God working through that person. We all need heroes and people to look up to and admire. These are our heroes in the faith.

Trust me, they all had their shortcomings and faults, but they persevered in spite of those faults. The second thing to remember is that as Catholics we believe that Christ gave St. Peter, our first Pope, the Keys of the Kingdom and authority that whatever he binds or looses on Earth is bound or loosed in Heaven (St. Matthew 18:18). We also believe that this authority has been passed down through the Papacy.

Let's look at a portion of Scripture in the New Testament that involves Old Testament believers. We consider the books of St. Matthew, St. Mark, St. Luke, and St. John part of the New Testament canon of Scripture; however, the events of all four of these books chronicle events taking place under the Old Covenant.

27. Some Sadducees, those who deny that there is a resurrection, came forward and put this question to him,

28. saying, "Teacher, Moses wrote for us, 'If someone's brother dies leaving a wife but no child, his brother must take the wife and raise up descendants for his brother.'

29. Now there were seven brothers; the first married a woman but died childless.

30. Then the second

31. and the third married her, and likewise all the seven died childless.

32. Finally the woman also died.

33. Now at the resurrection whose wife will that woman be? For all seven had been married to her."

34. Jesus said to them, "The children of this age marry and are given in marriage;

35. but those who are deemed worthy to attain to the coming age and to the resurrection of the dead neither marry nor are given in marriage.

36. They can no longer die, for they are like angels; and they are the children of God because they are the ones who will rise.

37. That the dead will rise even Moses made known in the passage about the bush, when he called 'Lord' the God of Abraham, the God of Isaac, and the God of Jacob;

38. and he is not God of the dead, but of the living, for to him all are alive."

39. Some of the scribes said in reply, "Teacher, you have answered well."

40. And they no longer dared to ask him anything.

St. Mark 12:27-40

The Jews in the passage above were not clear about the dead believers being alive. Jesus is very clear about the fact that Abraham, Isaac, and Jacob are very much alive. Let's look at another New Testament verse that involves Moses. It is one thing to understand in your mind that those who are with Christ are alive, and it is altogether another to believe with our hearts.

28. About eight days after he said this, he took Peter, John, and James and went up the mountain to pray.

29. While he was praying his face changed in appearance and his clothing became dazzling white.

30. And behold, two men were conversing with him, Moses and Elijah.

31. who appeared in glory and spoke of his exodus that he was going to accomplish in Jerusalem.

32. Peter and his companions had been overcome by sleep, but becoming fully awake, they saw his glory and the two men standing with him.

St. Luke 9:28-32

In this event chronicled by St. Luke and often referred to as *"the Mount of Transfiguration,"* the writer very clearly says that Jesus was conversing with Moses and Elijah. He doesn't say *"something that looked like Moses and Elijah"* or even *"a vision of Moses of Elijah."* He is very clear that the two talking with Jesus are, in fact, Moses and Elijah.

Let's look at another place in scripture where God very clearly shows us that believers do not die when their flesh stops working.

8. So he disguised himself (King Saul), putting on other clothes, and set out with two companions. They came to the woman at night, and Saul said to her, "Divine for me; conjure up the spirit I tell you."

9. But the woman answered him, "You know what Saul has done, how he expelled the mediums and diviners from the land. Then why are you trying to entrap me and get me killed?"

10. But Saul swore to her by the LORD, "As the LORD lives, you shall incur no blame for this."

11. "Whom do you want me to conjure up?" the woman asked him. "Conjure up Samuel for me," he replied.

12. When the woman saw Samuel, she

shrieked at the top of her voice and said to Saul, "Why have you deceived me? You are Saul!"

13. But the king said to her, "Do not be afraid. What do you see?" "I see a god rising from the earth," she replied.

14."What does he look like?" asked Saul. "An old man is coming up wrapped in a robe," she replied. Saul knew that it was Samuel, and so he bowed his face to the ground in homage.

15. Samuel then said to Saul, "Why do you disturb me by conjuring me up?" Saul replied: "I am in great distress, for the Philistines are waging war against me and God has turned away from me. Since God no longer answers me through prophets or in dreams, I have called upon you to tell me what I should do."

16. To this Samuel said: "But why do you ask me, if the LORD has abandoned you for your neighbor?

17. The LORD has done to you what he declared through me: he has torn the kingdom from your hand and has given it to your neighbor David.

18. "Because you disobeyed the LORD's di-

rective and would not carry out his fierce anger against Amalek, the LORD has done this to you today.

19. Moreover, the LORD will deliver Israel, and you as well, into the hands of the Philistines. By tomorrow you and your sons will be with me, and the LORD will have delivered the army of Israel into the hands of the Philistines."

1 Samuel 28:8-19

There are a few things worthy of mention concerning this section of scripture. The women, or medium, who contacts Samuel is often referred to as *"the Witch of Endor."* The scripture very clearly states that she *"conjured up Samuel,"* not a familiar spirit who looks like Samuel. This is Samuel! Notice that Samuel very clearly recognizes Saul, and not only does he very clearly recognize Saul, but he is also very clearly concerned about the situation that he has been called upon to address. This is not someone who has been awakened out of a sound sleep; this cowboy has his boots on, his wits about him, and is ready for action. Samuel prophesies to Saul concerning Israel being handed over to the Philistines. Samuel, even without his body, is still operating in the office of a prophet. Imagine that! (Pardon the sarcasm. His ministry did not end when his body died.)

I find great humor in this portion of scripture. It is no secret that King Saul was a bit of a thorn in the prophet Samuel's side. King Saul was one of those individuals who felt that the rules applied to everyone else but himself. He thought he could do exactly what he wanted to do, contrary to God's direction, and still be blessed. He just didn't seem to understand that his responsibility as King was to listen to God and obey. We have all been guilty of not listening to God from time to time. I know that for me, this behavior is very relatable.

I can imagine that on several occasions Samuel's eyes rolled back in his head, and he uttered a sigh of frustration in dealing with Saul. This is a perfect example of our seemingly incessant, impatient, behavior in wanting the blessings of God in our own time, instead of being content with what we have received, and waiting for His perfect will to unfold in our lives. To make things worse, while in the midst of reaping the undesirable fruits of our impatient behavior, we have the audacity to look towards Heaven and wonder why God has turned His back on us (as we perceive, not in reality), by not blessing us in our disobedience.

This scene is a good example of this human dilemma. Saul knows perfectly well that consulting with a witch goes completely against God's will; verse 9 above is evidence that he, himself, outlawed *"mediums and diviners from the land."* He so desperately wants God's blessing after having screwed up royally (pun intended), and now, in his mind, he is going to break his own law, which also happens to be one of God's rules, to receive a blessing from God.

I do not believe Samuel was in any way under the power of this medium to appear. I believe that Samuel wanted to appear. I picture the scene something like this. Samuel and God are watching this scene unfold from over the Balcony of Heaven. Consider that Saul got himself into the trouble he is in for not listening to Samuel when he was alive in the first place. I am sure that there is nothing more frustrating as a prophet than to stick you neck out to speak God's word and be completely ignored by its intended recipient when it does not suit the hearer's agenda.

We all would love a word from the Lord concerning our lives, but typically only if it speaks of a blessing that fits into our plans. Samuel looks over at God and gives him the nod *like "I got this one."* No words are needed between the two; they are on the same page. Samuel doesn't even bother to take the time to take the stairs. He leaps over the handrail, vaulting himself onto the scene with one arm. Look at verse 17, basically, what he is saying to Saul is *"Remember what I told you when I was alive and in your presence when we were face-to-face? What in the world would make you think that anything has changed, especially after this act of disobedience?"* Samuel, I believe, used great restraint by sticking to the script. I probably would have started out the conversation with *"Hey, thickhead."* That's me - *"Just keep'n it real."* (I hate that phrase, but it works.) I am still a work in progress that needs a lot of work. I am fairly confident that God has thought of my behavior from time to time in the same way.

Here is another rabbit trail but something to think about for those who think that praying to Saints is a waste of time. Samuel's hope was in Jesus while he walked the earth and in the flesh. Do you think when he met Jesus face-to-face in the spirit that he might have joined Jesus in what was important to Jesus, making sure that you and I make it to Heaven? I have no doubt that there is an endless sea of little old, blue-haired women with rosary beads in their hands not giving God a moment's rest, praying to Him for their children. Could a mother stop praying for her children? A mother's most important office of ministry is for her children.

I am sure that mothers get more persistent with praying for their children when they reach Heaven. All they will be thinking about is, *"When is Johnny coming home?"* I know in our home when one of our children is coming for the weekend, that is all that my wife thinks about for two weeks or longer before the visit. The house is cleaned several times, beds are prepared, and the refrigerator is packed to its fullest capacity.

I can just imagine the scene in Heaven, and all those mothers have no need for sleep! To be honest, the thought of the scene can be a little scary. I know that during those two weeks before one of my children arrive, my honey-do list grows exponentially. I love it when my children come, but some of the things my wife expects me to do to get ready are a little over the top, just like a mother's heart (over the top for her children). There is no saying no to my wife during preparation mode. If it is in her mind, it is going to happen. We men probably need to be praying for Jesus and, in an effort of solidarity, go easy on Him by staying out of trouble.

The Word of God very clearly teaches that the faithful do not die. Those who put their hope in Christ will live on forever with God in His Kingdom. When we become Christians, we receive the Spirit of Life and become hidden in Christ (Colossians 3:3). This is one of the mysteries of the Church. If we are going to pray for someone who has died to this life, the first hurdle we must jump is the belief that that person is alive in the spirit. When we die, all that changes is that our bodies hit the ground, and we become spiritually-minded, seeing with our spiritual eyes.

I believe it will be like waking from a dream. Our position in Christ and our position within our families do not change. When I die, I will still be the father of five children and a grandfather of who knows how many grandchildren. I am currently the proud grandfather of nine, but I am fairly confident there will be more before I pass on to live fully in the spirit. I understand that the scripture says that we will not be married, but will still be in relationship with one another within the Body of Christ, as one Body. I know that I keep skirting around the word *"die"* or dead. I am doing this in this writing to communicate a truth, but there is nothing wrong with saying that someone is dead. If a person is dead to his or her fleshly senses, his or her body is dead.

In my simple mind, I do not understand why praying for someone would make one bit of difference in whether or not they would be healed. Does God somehow need the energy from our prayers to work His healing mojo? Once again, I am being completely absurd to communicate a point. The fact is that God does not need help from us to do anything. God wants us to be involved in one another's lives. He wants us to be so over-the-top in love with Jesus and with our brothers and sisters that we passionately do whatever it takes to see them healed when they are sick or hurting. This is part of suffering with Christ. We should draw so close to Jesus and be so filled with His Spirit that, when we see another person in pain, our hearts ache in pain over his or her suffering.

I must admit that I am not even close to being where I want to be when it comes to praying for others. I am not even close to being where I want to be when it comes to praying, period. I have this great fantasy, as I am sure many others have, of being able to pray for hours on end like St. Teresa of Avila. I am a long way off, but day-by-day I will keep pressing into the Heart of Jesus. If we want to have more passion for praying for others and loving others, we need to love Jesus more. That's how it works. Love is a fruit of the Spirit, not of our hearts. Husbands, do you want to love your wives more? Chase after Jesus! Fall helplessly in love with Jesus, and you will love your wife the way you should. Nobody loves your wife more than Jesus does, and if you are filled with His Spirit, you will learn to see her through His Eyes and love her as He does. This goes for all of our relationships in this life and the life to come.

> *16. Therefore, confess your sins to one another and pray for one another, that you may be healed. The fervent prayer of a righteous person is very powerful.*
>
> *James 5:16*

Here is the big question. If we have a loved one who dies and there is any chance that he or she is laying on the banks of the *"river of life-giving water, sparkling like crystal, flowing from the throne of God and of the Lamb"* (Revelation 22:1), being nurtured by *"the leaves of the trees serve as medicine for the nations"* (Revelation 22:2), why would you not be praying for that person?

As Catholics, the answer is simple. We would be praying for that person! Catholics commonly ask others to pray for the *"repose"* of the soul of a loved one who has passed away. The word *"repose"* simply means to be at rest or peace. So, in other words, they ask for prayer that the person that has passed away be healed of all of the hurts carried over from this world.

Protestants, the Scripture is very clear concerning healing taking place in Heaven. You will need to search your hearts. The word Purgatory is not in the Bible, but as we have discussed, evidence of its existence is indisputable regardless of what it is called. There are a couple of instances recorded in Scripture of people praying for the dead, but they are nothing that I would ever suggest that anyone use as precedent for praying for the dead. There are many good reasons for praying for the dead, but just because someone else has done it is not a good reason for us to follow in the practice.

If you died right now, are you ready to be presented as the Bride of Christ dressed in pure white without spot or blemish? I know I am not. I am not even close. Just this morning during Mass, our pastor said something that touched a hidden wound. The more I press into God, the more I understand that I am in desperate need of His healing touch.

My Protestant and Catholic brothers and sisters, please pray for me when I pass from this life. Pray that I will meet my uncle along the banks of the River of Life. Pray that God will heal me of all of the hurts that I have suffered during my journey upon the Earth. Please pray that I will have the opportunity to face all of the people whom I have hurt along the way.

> *2. There is nothing concealed that will not be revealed, nor secret that will not be known.*
>
> *3. Therefore whatever you have said in the darkness will be heard in the light, and what you have whispered behind closed doors will be proclaimed on the housetops.*

> *St. Luke 12:2-3*

Every sin will be revealed in Heaven. Yes, even yours, and even mine. God is not holding those sins against us, nor is He exposing those sins as punishment. Rather, Jesus is saying this to let people who think that they have gotten away with being unkind to others know that they are mistaken. He is saying, *"Think before you act because you will be held accountable for the sake of the person you hurt."*

If I have hurt you during this life, I am truly sorry. Please come to me and let me know if it is reasonably possible. There are things that will not be set right in this life; people's lives change. When we come to Christ, we will inevitably look back at our lives and understand that we have hurt others. We may be able to approach some of those people and ask for forgiveness, but there will be some whom we should be sensitive enough of concerning their current circumstances to leave things alone and trust that God will work everything out in His perfect time.

A person's guilty conscience is no excuse for compounding the pain of a past sin by carelessly barging into someone's life where you will most likely be unwelcome. If you are unable to do so in this life, wait until the next. I will wait along the banks of the River of Life for as long as it takes for whomever it may be that God knows that I need to set things right with. I am in no hurry; I will be there if it takes two months, a thousand years, or longer. When we enter the Father's presence, presented by Christ as His Bride, all things will be set right. For the believer, every hurt will be healed.

4. He will wipe every tear from their eyes, and there shall be no more death or mourn-

ing, wailing or pain, [for] the old order has passed away."

Revelation 21:4

When we learn to adopt an eternal perspective, time changes. I know it has for me. At times, if I am not careful, time starts to fly by, but for the most part, my perception of time is that it has slowed. I am beginning to understand that I do not need to be in a hurry all of the time, especially when it comes to my eternal future. I am starting to understand that I do not need to *"have it all together"* before I die. This is not an excuse not to work hard at becoming Holy, but it is an understanding that it is not me who makes me Holy—an understanding that I cannot control (or a better word might be *"influence"*) anything in my life other than the moment I am in right now. We need to learn to live fully in every moment. I am starting to have the feeling that if we grab ahold of God tightly enough that time could stand still.

When will we come to a place in this life when we are completely content with Christ and Christ alone? Think about it; we have everything we need from God. We could do nothing more to make Him love us any more than He already does. We have everything from God that we will ever need to receive. We have it all. Think about that. What else could God give us that we need that we don't already have? Why don't we feel it? Why don't we believe it? Why are we always looking for more? Why are we in such a hurry? To get where? And for what? People long for the time when they will be in God's presence and worship Him forever. Get started! You are in His presence; you can start worshiping Him with your life right now. What are you waiting for? *"Let the dead bury their own dead"* and follow Him (St. Matthew 8:22). The key to understanding anything that I have written above is to need Jesus Christ and Him alone.

We need to understand that anything other than Jesus Christ that we hang on to in this life, as St. Paul would say, is garbage (Philippians 3:8). As Jesus told the Pharisees in St. Mark chapter 2, verses 27 and 28, *"The Sabbath was made for man, not man for the Sabbath. That is why the Son of Man is lord even of the Sabbath."* Likewise, Purgatory is for man, and Jesus is the Lord of our healing. Jesus takes the time to heal us, not because He needs it or requires it of us. Yes, he does require that we forgive one another, but that is because He loves us and will not stand by and watch us hurt one another or ourselves. I wish I could just let go of all of the pain that disrupts my life - the Lord knows I have tried to give it totally to Him - but I can't do it, and He understands that. My kids all make fun of me, in love, of course, because they will look over at me during a television commercial and I will be crying. The pain that is set so deep within our souls will only be healed by His touch. I believe that there are some wounds that will never be healed in this life, but we will learn to walk in perfect love with those wounds bound by His grace. Jesus takes the time to heal us purely out of His love for us.

Don't look at purgation or time in Purgatory as something to dread. Look at it as a time of being loved by Christ. I think that one of the reasons that people do not want to accept that Purgatory exists is because they are in too much of a hurry to get into the Throne Room of Heaven; they want everything right now. Slow down. If you are in Christ, the Throne Room of God belongs to you. It is your irrevocable inheritance. It has always existed and it always will. You will see it soon enough. Some may say that having such an eternal perspective is dangerous, causing laziness and eliminating the need to prepare for Heaven. I know for me it has caused just the opposite. It has given me the feeling, paradoxical to what I have written above, that I am preparing for a trip for which there is not nearly enough time to get ready. Time slows, but yet there is a real sense of purpose and direction. Are my children ready? How many of the hurting of this world can I be a part of snatching from the grip of the evil one? Time marches by, and not one single moment will ever be re-lived. We do not need to be in a hurry but focused on using every moment of every day wisely, being wise stewards of the time our Lord has blessed us with (St. Matthew 25:14-30).

I would encourage every believer to read *"Hinds' Feet on High Places"* written by Hannah Hurnard. The book in an allegorical tale chronicling the main character's, *"Much Afraid's,"* journey to the *"High Places."* She is watched over and guided by the shepherd whom she eventually meets in the High Places in a very unexpected way. The struggles, pain, and fear that she experiences along the way are very touching and also very relatable. Along her journey, Much Afraid would often become impatient with her progress, wanting to be further along the path on which she was being guided.

The first time that I read the book, I can remember being frustrated with Much Afraid's impatient behavior. I would say to myself, *"What is your hurry? You are on the journey of your life, and you are missing the beauty of the experi- ence with your incessant worrying."* At times, she would be led along a path that seemed to lead away from the mountain, but that after much time spent in frustration and needless worry, she would learn was a necessary part of the journey. I soon began to realize, as I turned the pages, that I was and still am in many ways just like Much Afraid in this regard. What's my hurry? I get to spend every moment of every day on this most amazing journey with our Lord right by my side. What could be better?

What I have been frantically searching for my entire life, I have living within me. Yes, I have suffered and will undoubtedly suffer some more, but I will also receive joy unspeakable in this life and in the life to come. I have a beautiful wife, five great children, nine grandchildren, who knows how many future grandchildren, with the way my children reproduce, and the promise of eternity with Jesus; life is good. One of the most exciting things about the journey is that we never know what is in store for us around the next bend, but that we do know that Jesus will be right by our side. The Lord is our portion; He is more than sufficient in all things. He is not only first in our lives; He is first in all things in our lives. He is The Lord of our marriages, Lord of our children, and, yes, Lord of our suffering hearts. In Christ alone, we live in all things.

Yes, please pray for me when I pass from this life, and, more importantly, please pray for the loved ones whom I leave behind. Please pray that I be healed, but please do not pray that I leave Purgatory one moment sooner than I should. I very selfishly want to spend every moment that I can in the healing Arms of Jesus.

Final Thoughts

~

*"Our souls demand Purgatory, don't they?
Would it not break the heart if God said to
us, 'It is true, my son, that your breath
smells and your rags drip with mud and
slime, but we are charitable here and no one
will upbraid you with these things, nor draw
away from you. Enter into the joy'? Should
we not reply, 'With submission, sir, and if
there is no objection, I'd rather be cleaned
first.' 'It may hurt, you know' - 'Even so, sir.'"*

C.S. Lewis, Letters To Malcolm: Chiefly on Prayer,
chapter 20, paragraphs 7-10, pages 108-109

The words *"Trinity"* and *"Incarnation"* are
not in the Bible, and both have caused debate
within the Church, but neither has caused division like the word *"Purgatory."* I think for the
most part this is because it deals with death and
suffering, both wildly unpopular topics of discussion within most social circles. This combined
with the gross misrepresentation by many
throughout the ages has made this division understandable. I shake my head as I consider that
the doctrine that I stood against with such disdain has become a wellspring of life within my

heart.

The biggest stumbling block to human development is expressed with two words, *"I understand."* To be convinced that we understand something completely is to shut our minds to learning. Yes, there is absolute truth, such as the Holiness of God and the Divinity of Christ, but to say that I understand God would be arrogant at the very least. My mind was closed concerning Purgatory. I was sure I understood. We do the same thing with people. How often do we say within our hearts, *"What a bum,"* when we see someone begging for money at the bottom of an exit ramp? I know I think it more often than not, to my shame. The truth is, I know nothing at all about the condition of another man's heart, and to make things even worse, I am learning more and more every day that I do not completely understand my own. The more honest we are with ourselves, the more we will come to understand that we understand very little.

It is right and good for us to study the Scripture. I would think a heart longing to know God would want to gain as much knowledge of the scripture as humanly possible. It is one thing to seek knowledge, but it is another to be puffed up with religious pride saying within our hearts that we understand. Consider the Pharisees during the time when Jesus physically walked amongst His people Israel. Many were blinded by the religious pride of believing they understood. And look at the Apostle Paul. Our Lord had to knock him off of his *"high horse"* and blind him by covering his eyes with scales (Acts 9:4). Many Bible scholars feel that it was unlikely that Paul was riding a horse, but I like the pun. Then he was led by the hand into Damascus, where God removed the scales covering his eyes at the laying on of the hands of Ananias. Prior to this event, Paul had been heading to Damascus to round up all of the Christians he could find to kill, most likely. Puffed up in religious pride, he thought he was doing God's work. God now had Paul, who at that time was named Saul, being healed by one of the ones whom he was headed to persecute. Don't you hate it when you are absolutely sure that you are right, without a doubt know that you are correct, only to find out that you are absolutely wrong? I wish I could say I have no idea how it feels, but, unfortunately, I can relate to the experience all too well.

Please, let me insert that it is not my intention for us to come to the point of ridiculousness concerning the word *"understand."* I am using the word to illustrate a point. I use the word very often, and in its proper context there is nothing wrong with saying *"I understand."* Sure as rain, someone reading this will say that Bill Novack said that we should never use the word *"understand."*

I have approached the Book of Revelation with much caution after learning from the example of the Pharisees at the time of Christ. The Book of Revelation is written in a kind of code often referred to as Apocalyptic. The first parts of the Bible written in this style were parts of the book of Denial during the Babylonian captivity. Many feel that prophets were given this type of prophetic message during times of captivity to offer words of warning as well as words of encouragement—God's way of communicating with His children during their time of need. Remember, at the time when the Apostle John wrote Revelation, Israel was under Roman rule. This may have been a way of being able to distribute the book (the message) throughout the Church, in a way that if Roman authorities found it, it would most likely be passed off as the rants of a madman.

It is very important that we gain as much knowledge as possible concerning this message from God (the book of Revelation) without becoming convinced that we *"understand"* its every meaning. Don't be so sure that we could not become modern day Pharisees by being proud of the fact that we completely understand this book and miss the signs of Christ's return. Trust me, there are countless books written on the subject of *"understanding Revelation."* The book of Revelation was written so we would be able to discern the times (St. Luke 12:56). We are to study the book, so when the events in the book take place, we will be able to understand what is happening. Many of the events, as believed by many, have already come to pass. If we are convinced we understand the book, we will most likely miss the events altogether.

How many of us draw a picture in our minds of the appearance of someone whom we have never met, only based on his or her voice on the radio or on the phone, only to find out that the individual looks nothing like what we had imagined? We as human beings so easily fall into the trap of associating past experiences with things that we deal with in the present. That person whom we talk to on the phone, whom we have never met, may sound like an old friend, so we draw a picture of that old friend in our minds. How many times do we meet someone who looks like someone we knew from the past and are a little taken aback when he or she does not act in the same way as our old acquaintance?

Sometimes God uses these past experiences to help us relate to what He is trying to say. Let's look at the passage from Revelation that we looked at in the first chapter of this book (Holiness).

1. Then the angel showed me the river of life giving water, sparkling like crystal, flowing from the throne of God and of the Lamb

2. down the middle of its street. On either side of the river grew the tree of life that produces fruit twelve times a year, once each month: the leaves of the trees serve as medicine for the nations.

3. Nothing accursed will be found there anymore. The throne of God and of the Lamb will be in it, and His servants will worship Him.

Revelation 22:1-3

What type of picture is God drawing in the mind of the reader and, most likely at the time when this book was written, in the mind of the listener? Most can relate to a river running with crystal clear water and banks that are lined with trees. What comes to my mind is a river in the

Carolina Mountains. Yes, it brings us to a *"place of peace and tranquility"* within our minds.

What truth is God communicating to His people, who are feeling very scared during their time of captivity? That He loves them—that what flows from Heaven is a river of His love and healing. He is telling them *"Do not worry, I have your healing all figured out."* He is saying to us, *"Just trust in me. Wade out into healing waters and become submersed in My love."* In other words, *"I love you. Relax and trust Me. I have this under control."*

What do we know for sure about the way this looks in Heaven? Not a thing! Nothing! Nada! Zilch! Zero! God is trying to communicate a spiritual truth by painting a physical picture within the minds of His people. I picture a river in the mountains with large live oak trees along its banks. Another might see a river on a tropical island lined with palm trees. Both visions are perfect as long as we understand what God is trying to relate—that He loves us and that He will heal us.

Let's take a look at a couple areas of Scripture that are often referred to by those trying to make a case for praying for those in Purgatory that we have not touched on during this discussion.

29. Otherwise, what will people accomplish by having themselves baptized for the dead? If the dead are not raised at all, then why are they having themselves baptized for them?

1 Corinthians 15:29

40. But under the tunic of each of the dead they found amulets sacred to the idols of Jamnia, which the law forbids the Jews to wear. So it was clear to all that this was why these men had fallen.

41. They all therefore praised the ways of the Lord, the just judge who brings to light the things that are hidden.

42. Turning to supplication, they prayed that the sinful deed might be fully blotted out.   The noble Judas exhorted the people to keep themselves free from sin, for they had seen with their own eyes what had happened because of the sin of those who had fallen.

43. He then took up a collection among all his soldiers, amounting to two thousand silver drachmas, which he sent to Jerusalem to provide for an expiatory sacrifice. In doing this he acted in a very excellent and noble way, inasmuch as he had the resurrection in mind;

44. for if he were not expecting the fallen to rise again, it would have been superfluous and foolish to pray for the dead.

45. But if he did this with a view to the splendid reward that awaits those who had gone to rest in godliness, it was a holy and pious thought.

46. Thus he made atonement for the dead that they might be absolved from their sin.

2 Maccabees 12:40-46

What truth can we glean from these two sections of Scripture? That the Jewish culture had a practice of interceding (praying, being baptized) on behalf of the dead. The Jews still to this day offer prayers for the dead.

What do we *"understand"* concerning the effectiveness of praying for the dead? The answer is very little or nothing. We would like to think it helps, but we have absolutely no evidence that it does. However, it is never wrong to intercede for another out of love and compassion.

I must say a word to my Catholic brothers and sisters concerning these two verses. Reciting these two verses in defense of your belief in Purgatory is an incomplete answer in the mind of a Protestant. Please do not take offense to what I am saying. My heart in this is to attempt to begin to chip away at some of the walls that so needlessly divide. The Protestant movement was birthed out of such a defensive posture that skepticism has become deeply ingrained within her fabric. You would sooner get green out of grass than remove skepticism from a Protestant. I am not saying this as a negative thing, and I doubt that a Protestant reading this has been insulted. I know because I am this way. I began my faith journey in the Protestant Church, and I am glad of it. When I went through RCIA (Right of Christian Initiation of Adults), as I entered the Catholic Church, quite often I went home and sifted through the scripture. On one side of my Bible was the Strong's Concordance and on the other the Interlinear Bible. I researched everything that I was being taught.

I believe that the Protestant Church has been a very needed tool for the Church as a whole for its good. The Protestant Church has brought about good within the Catholic Church that would have never happened if not for Her existence. Protestants may be feisty skeptics, but Catholics are hard-headed in other ways. Protestants want to know why. Just because someone prayed for the dead in the Bible is not enough. Not to mention that as soon as most

Protestants have been old enough to listen, they have heard arguments as to why these two portions of Scripture are wrongly interpreted by the Catholic Church. Catholics, type in *"praying for the dead"* in the Google search bar on your computer and you will be able to read plenty of these arguments.

Catholics, it is not enough to just recite scripted answers. We need to start reaching out with our hearts. We need to start reaching across the line that has divided for way too long. I have walked in both camps; our differences are not that great. Both traditions love Jesus in the same passionate way but express themselves in a slightly different manner.

We know so very little about ourselves. What makes us think that we have any right to judge another?

Before I share my favorite scripture passages that I feel point toward our Father's healing in Heaven, I would like to share an event that happened to me over 25 years ago. Let me preface this account by saying that God spoke to me deeply through this event, but in no way do I feel that it was orchestrated by Him. God never causes harm but can bring good out of the worst of circumstances.

In the mid-90s, I worked as a tractor trailer driver. One morning, I was driving down the interstate and a van coming in the opposite direction swerved out of control and rolled across the median. The median was a wide expanse of grass that was probably 100-feet wide. I had to stop to keep from hitting the van as it came to rest about 100 feet in front of my truck. When I jumped down out of my truck, I started running towards the van. It was not until I was about halfway there that I noticed that there was a man lying in the road. Up until this point, things had happened very fast. It had only been 30 seconds from when I first noticed the van swerving. I had been operating on pure instinct, but now time came to a crawl. The next 15 to 20 minutes before the paramedics arrived on the scene seemed like they lasted for three hours.

This is the type of scene that every person who spends any time on the interstate prays they never witnesses. In an attempt to spare all of the uncomfortable details, when I came to a stop, I was looking down at a man who was, simply put, *"broken."* All of my EMT training was not going to help this man no matter how hard I tried. I knelt at this man's side and tried to do something to help him while several people were yelling, *"Stop there is nothing you can do!"* So I did all I knew to do. While on my knees, I grabbed ahold of his arm and prayed for him until the paramedics arrived.

Once the paramedics arrived, I stepped to the side and watched. While I was standing there, a police officer walked over to me and started asking me questions. He had a clipboard in his hand, which had the driver's license of the man whom I had been praying for tucked in under the clip. I was shocked to see my neighbor's picture when I looked at the license. I did not know this person very well, but he was someone whom I waved to or said hello to several times a week. Our children were friends, and they lived right around the corner on the next street.

The officer could obviously see the look on my face because he asked me if I was okay and if I needed to sit down. I explained to the officer that I had been kneeling over this man for 20 minutes and had not recognized him, but that he was my neighbor. I answered a few more questions and started walking towards my truck when the officer came running after me to be sure that I was okay. I told him that I just needed to drive a few miles to the terminal and that I thought I would be fine.

I arrived at the terminal a little shaken but

able to function. I turned in my paperwork, got in my car, and drove home. I felt fine, and now that I think back on the situation, a little too fine. I walked through the front door of my house and my wife, Mary, asked me with a look of concern what was wrong. I obviously did not look as fine as I felt.

As soon as I started telling Mary what had happened, I came undone. I began to shake and sob uncontrollably. I can remember being taken completely off guard by my emotions. Now that I have had time to reflect on the situation, my wife had become a place of safety for me in a time of *"great distress."* I have obviously built defense mechanisms within my subconscious mind to keep me functioning until I can find my way to a safe place. My wife, Mary, is that safe place for me. She is my best friend on earth, and during that time, she was very much Christ to me. Jesus was right there by my side ministering to me through my wife.

One day, we will pass from this life through the Door into Heaven (St. John 10-9) and Jesus will be waiting to greet us with open arms of safety. I have imagined the scene many times. Looking into the Eyes of Jesus and feeling His embrace, the feeling of complete safety, overwhelmed with joy, knowing that the journey is over. I can then envision collapsing at His feet as all of the pain of this life of distress begins to surface. All of the hurts and burdens that we may not even be - no, most likely are not - aware of that we are carrying around are unloaded at His feet. He will kneel down, meet us where we are at, and put His arms around us for as long as needed.

> *3. I heard a loud voice from the throne saying, "Behold, God's dwelling is with the human race. He will dwell with them and they will be his people and God himself will always be with them [as their God].*
>
> *4. He will wipe every tear from their eyes, and there shall be no more death or mourning, wailing or pain, [for] the old order has passed away."*
>
> *Revelation 21:3-4*

> *13. Then one of the elders spoke up and said to me, "Who are these wearing white robes, and where did they come from?"*
>
> *14. I said to him, "My lord, you are the one who knows." He said to me, "These are the ones who have survived the time of **great distress**; they have washed their robes and*

made them white in the blood of the Lamb. "For this reason they stand before God's throne and worship him day and night in his temple. The one who sits on the throne will shelter them.

16. They will not hunger or thirst anymore, nor will the sun or any heat strike them.

17. For the Lamb who is in the center of the throne will shepherd them and lead them to springs of life-giving water, and God will wipe away every tear from their eyes."

Revelation 7:13-17

Our souls not only *"demand purgatory"*; it is promised.

This is what I do know to be irrefutably true about what the Bible teaches about Jesus and Purgatory. It is that if we keep our eyes on the goal, who is Jesus, receiving Him as Lord and Savior, that He is faithful and just to forgive us of our sins (1 John 9) and that He is waiting for us here in this life, as well as in Heaven, with open arms where He will wipe away our every tear and heal us from the pain that we have suffered during this *"time of great distress"* (Revelation 7:14).

Footnotes

~

1. When I use the label of *"Catholic"* or *"Protestant,"* I can only speak from my personal experience within both camps. I understand that all Protestants do not believe, exactly, in the same way, any more than all Catholics believe in the same way. Within the Protestant faith, there are many different churches expressing themselves in different ways, while in the Catholic Church, we too have many people expressing themselves in different ways within the same church. There are charismatic Catholics just as there are charismatic Protestants, likewise conservatives, likewise those that some would consider liberal, and so on.

2. I understand that seeing the Holy Spirit referred to as *"She"* may be a little odd. Many writers will refer to the Holy Spirit as *"He"* or *"It"*. There are countless writings and debates concerning which is correct. The words for Holy Spirit in both the Hebrew language of the Old Testament (Ruach HaKadosh) and in the Aramaic language (Ruha d'qudsha) that Jesus spoke are written in the feminine.

God is *"Spirit"*, and most Bible scholars agree that God most likely does not have a gender. Unfortunately, during this life, we are limited to communicating with the written and spoken word. If the Hebrew Authors of the Old Testament feel that the Holy Spirit is feminine, I feel it important that we will follow in their tradition.

3. For our Protestant readers, a brief explanation will be helpful here. For a more detailed understanding look up *"Hesychasm"*. This is a very old and very orthodox form of prayer or meditation. Through the ages, the Church has developed methods of prayer called meditation and contemplation. They are two different acts but go hand in hand, like the ebb and flow of the tides. During this meditation (the outgoing tide) a small portion of scripture is repeated over and over and meditated on until it becomes a rhythm in the heart. The particular prayer that I reference is the *"Jesus Prayer"* or the *"Kyrie Eleison."* Both of these prayers have their origin from St. Luke 18:13 where the tax collector *"stood off at a distance and would not even raise his eyes to heaven but beat his breast and prayed, 'O God, be merciful to me a sinner'"*. Some people actually will pat their chest dur-

ing the prayer in memory of God's word. This is a meditation on humility, to remember how much we are in need of Jesus. I understand that these two prayers are structured as prayers of petition, but they in actuality are prayed more in the spirit of communion, with an emphasis of relating to God our awareness of our own sinfulness. In other words, the person praying is not literally praying over and over again in petition for forgiveness, but more as a way of settling within the heart the reality of our reliance on the grace of God in an act humility. Any portion of scripture can be used or some just focus on things like God's divinity or the passion of Christ. Very often I just repeat over and over in my heart the words *"Jesus you are Lord."*

During contemplation (the incoming tide) the believer quiets the mind and listens for what God has to say in return.

Please do not confuse this contemplation with the new age contemplative or centering prayer that is becoming very popular in both Catholic and Protestant circles. For a better understanding of meditation and contemplation, I would recommend reading St. Teresa of Avila's writing titled the *"Interior Castle."*

This is a book that new age spiritualists love to quote but, based on their actions, clearly, do not understand.

4. The translators of the New American Bible, Revised Edition (NABRE) included what in most translations would be the last two verses of chapter 1 at the beginning of chapter 2. The text reads the same but what would be verse 23 in the majority of translations is verse 25 above.

5. I understand that the sacrament of Reconciliation, or better known as *"Confession,"* is a little foreign to our Protestant brothers and sisters. Most are likely thinking at this point, *"Why do Catholics feel that they need to go to a priest to be forgiven? Why don't they just go directly to Jesus?"* This subject would involve the addition of several chapters to this book, which would be a little off subject. However, I would like to include the following to explain why the sacrament has become so important in my life.

To begin with, I don't believe that we will be able to understand the need for confession until we begin to understand Our Father's Heart for us, His children. The sad thing about this is that there are plenty of Catholics who go to Confession out of religious guilt, while missing the real power of the sacrament. Trust me, the ministry of guilt is alive and well in the Catholic Church, just as it is in the Protestant Church. There are plenty of priests who like to preach condemnation, just as there are Protestant preachers who like to preach hellfire and brimstone.

I can't help but think of the movie *Fiddler on the Roof*. For those who have not watched the movie, the setting is in the small village of Anatevka, Russia in the year 1905. It is a musical that depicts a Jewish father, Tevye, as he struggles between his Jewish traditions and the progressive thinking that is starting to take hold among the younger generation concerning marriage. In his Jewish tradition, marriages are arranged by matchmakers. His daughters would like to marry for love. His oldest daughter, Tzeitel, arranged by her father to marry a man in their village, pleads that she be allowed to marry out of love rather than out of the Jewish tradition of matchmaking. Tevye's heart is melted out of love for his daughter, and he allows her to marry the young man who she loves within the Jewish faith.

However, his younger daughter, Hodel, takes this dilemma to a much higher level. She falls in love with a Marxist revolutionary. She has not only stepped out of bounds as to what is acceptable within Jewish tradition; she has furthermore fallen in love with a Marxist, who are the cause of much of the Jewish suffering in the region. Tevye shuns his daughter and will not even speak to her. She moves out of the house, banished from the family in shame. During one of the very last scenes of the movie, the Jews in the village are ordered to leave the country by the Marxists, and Tevye's daughter pleads with him to acknowledge her. She just so desperately wants to know that he loves her. Tevye will not even look at her, and he gets busy securing the cart that he will need to pull with all of his family's belongings. Finally, Hodel gives up and begins to walk away with her husband. The scene is absolutely heartbreaking. But then it happens, Tevye very quietly utters a blessing over his daughter.

Through the struggle within the heart of this man emerges the truth of why Tevye is so upset. When everything was said and done, the reason Tevye was crushed in spirit over this issue was that he knew that her decisions would cause the inevitable separation between his daughter and himself. But, in the end, his father's heart won the day, out of love. Yes, his heart was crushed, but it fought its way through all of the confusion and acted out in love by going against the very tradition that had dictated every part of his life. Tevye truly had the heart of a *"papa."*

This story of Tevye and his daughter is the perfect example of the gospel message of Grace. The Law kills if followed to the letter. Tevye by all rights and according to The Law he lived by should have never spoken to his daughter again. The results of her transgression was separation from the Jewish community, and most importantly for this analogy, from her father, but the grace of this man ministered life, just as our Father in Heaven has resurrected us to new life through His loving grace by the Blood of His Son Jesus. His heart is devastated over our brokenness, and the thought of us being separated from Him is obviously beyond what He is willing to live with.

We need to understand that it is unlikely that our Father in Heaven is sitting on His Throne pissed off and feeling disrespected because of our sin. The sin in which we are entangled breaks our Father's heart because He knows that it will inevitably drive a wedge of separation between His children and Himself. This is not saying that God does not rightfully expect our respect. We must never lose sight of the fact that He is God and deserves our utmost respect.

I don't believe that our Father is sitting in Heaven freaked out about our sin, because, as I said above, that we have somehow disrespected Him; He knows the struggles that we face every day during this life. He knows that with sin comes shame, and with shame comes separation from Him.

Look at Adam and Eve in the garden. What happened when they sinned? Yes, they hid from God out of shame for what they had done.

Let me tell you the real reason why I believe people have such a hard time with Confession. It is because people are afraid of the shame of judgment. People are afraid of other people thinking that they are less than perfect. I am one of those people. I have considered going to another parish, possibly to another state, to go to Confession so that I don't have to sit in front of my pastor and tell him that I did the same stupid thing that I did the last time we talked. I have this picture in my mind, just before going to Confession, of the priest hearing my confession and picking up a big stick from behind his chair and beating me to a pulp while saying something along the lines of *"You stupid, stupid, idiot. You are as dumb as a rock. Now get out, and don't come back, you piece of excrement."* I can promise you that has never happened, not even close.

Herein lies the power of Confession. My vision of the priest beating me and the words I imagine him speaking of me are all things that I think of myself. Time and time again, I have fallen into sin giving the enemy of our souls, the devil, Lucifer, who was cast out of Heaven in a bitter seething hatred, the accuser of the brethren (Revelation 12: 10), the perfect opportunity to torment me in an attempt to separate me from God forever, with words like *"You stupid, stupid, idiot."* This is why we so desperately need to strip the enemy of his power and go to Confession. This is when Jesus, through the priest (in Persona Christi), tells us, *"Don't listen to the lies of the enemy. You are not a piece of excrement;*

you are My beloved. Yes, you have sinned, but I forgive you, and I love you, and I always will. You are fearfully and wonderfully made [Psalm 139:14]. You are always welcome in My Kingdom. We will get through this together. Now 'go and sin no more [St. John 8:11]. I am faithful to complete the good work that I have started in you [Philippians 1:6].' " Of course, I am paraphrasing; I have never had a priest use these exact words, but I assure you that this is exactly the truth that Jesus is communicating during the sacrament.

There is something truly powerful about looking someone in the eye, confessing the sins that torment, and hearing the words *"you are forgiven."* Trust me, at times it takes everything within me to walk through the doors of my pastor's office for Confession and tell him of the shameful things that I have done. Imagine if Jesus appeared before us and we had to confess to Him, face-to-face. Please do not take this the wrong way. It may sound all well and good to go into a closet and confess your sins to Jesus, but if you were looking him in the eye, it would be a different matter. I am not saying this would be a bad thing; what I am saying is that I am not sure that I could even speak. I have a hard time telling a priest about my sins. I could not imagine how difficult it would be to tell Jesus face-to-face.

For me, in my life, the accountability and personal touch involved in the sacrament has been life changing. It is way different looking someone in the eye. With pride comes shame; the two are inseparable. Humility is the instrument used to expose the shame hidden by pride. When we confess our sins to another, it exposes that shame that keeps us from turning our faces upward fully toward God. This is not a concept known only to Catholics. Many overcomer's groups use the concept of accountability partners: alcoholics anonymous, many sexual addiction counseling programs, and many Protestant ministry groups.

Let me also make perfectly clear, I am not in any way saying that if someone is not Catholic - if he or she does not go to Confession - that Jesus does not forgive that person of his or her sins. I am simply explaining why I choose to take part in the Sacrament of Reconciliation. God works through the sacraments; He is not bound by the sacraments. Faith in Jesus Christ alone is where we find salvation. We are saved by faith in Jesus Christ, not by the Catholic Church. We are not to ever judge another man's servant (Romans 14:4).

End Notes

~

If anyone one would like to reach out to me with questions concerning this book, about the Catholic Church, or to sign to subscribe to my mailing list, please contact through my web-site at www.wjnovack.com, or e-mail me at bill@wjnovack.com.

Being or becoming Catholic, as many have experienced, is wonderful, but can also be very frustrating. I love being Catholic, but the Church is a very old establishment full of some very odd and different beliefs. Many of these beliefs have nothing to do with growing closer to God and living the sacramental life of The Church but are taught by many within The Church as if they do (Clergy or Laity). We as Catholics believe that The Church is the *"pillar and foundation of truth" (Timothy 3:15)*, but it is perfectly acceptable to ask questions, especially when something is not sitting right within your conscience. Learn to ask why. It may just be the *"small, still voice"* of the Holy Spirit.

I do not work for the Catholic Church, nor am I a Priest, but I will be glad to help in any way that I can.

39481605R00144

Made in the USA
Middletown, DE
16 January 2017